A PLUM

YOU BL

T0176196

Mindy Tucker

Greg Haerling

JOSH GONDELMAN is a comedian and writer who incubated in Boston before moving to New York. He currently writes for *Last Week Tonight with John Oliver*, which is a television show. He has also written for *Women's Health*, *The New Yorker*, and *The Cut*, which are magazines. He has toured internationally performing stand-up, which is just heavily rehearsed talking, really.

JOE BERKOWITZ is a writer living in Brooklyn. His work has been featured in The Awl, Salon, *The Village Voice*, *Cosmopolitan*, Vulture, *Rolling Stone*, *GQ*, and McSweeney's Internet Tendency, among others. He is currently a staff editor at Fast Company. He apologizes in advance and often.

YOU BLEW IT!

AN
AWKWARD
LOOK AT
THE MANY WAYS
IN WHICH
YOU'VE ALREADY
RUINED
YOUR LIFE

JOSH GONDELMAN
and
JOE BERKOWITZ

A PLUME BOOK

Plume
An imprint of Penguin Random House LLC
375 Hudson Street
New York, New York 10014

Copyright ©2016 by Josh Gondelman and Joe Berkowitz

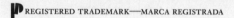

REGISTERED TRADEMARK—MARCA REGISTRADA

Library of Congress Cataloging-in-Publication Data
was applied for.

Printed in the United States of America
1   3   5   7   9   10   8   6   4   2

For Nana Kay, who always seemed skeptical I'd finish this thing. (JG)

For Mom, Dad, and Gabi, who deserve better but seldom complain. (JB)

CONTENTS

Welcome to the Working Weak

You're Going Places (at Least, Physically)

ACKNOWLEDGMENTS

This book would not be possible without the tireless shepherding of Noah Ballard at Curtis Brown and the enthusiastic championing of Matthew Daddona at Plume. Those two guys really wanted to see *You Blew It!* come together, and that's mainly why it did. Emma Sweeney was instrumental as well, and we owe a big loving embrace to the entire team at Plume.

From Josh Gondelman:

I'd like to extend deep and sincere thanks to the following people for the following reasons:

To my mom and dad for being fully supportive of my creative endeavors as long as they provided me health care. To my sister Jenna for being the actual best sibling and also for going halves on birthday gifts for my parents during my years of wild nonsuccess. To Maris for encouraging me, but more important for inspiring me by setting an example for a brilliant dedicated professional and human. To the grandparents, aunts, uncles, and cousins who have always cheered me on and who've even stopped asking, "You make a living at that?" To Chenoa, Tiffany, Taryn, and Marcus for being pals and being world-beaters. To all the great writing instructors I had at Brandeis for cultivating my silly jokes into complete sentences. To the comedy communities of Boston and New York for not putting up with any crap. And to the Arlington Infant Toddler Center for putting up with all of my crap.

From Joe Berkowitz:

Large swaths of this book were written in the following locations: Breukelen Coffee House in Crown Heights, Whole Foods in Tribeca, Aroma Espresso Bar on Church Street, and Starbucks on Chambers Street. Thanks to the supreme leniency of my editor at Fast Company, Teressa Iezzi, for giving me time to work on this book. Thanks to Gabriele O'Connor, my moon and stars, who gave invaluable feedback and encouragement throughout the whole process and beyond. Howard Berkowitz and Risé Page were nothing but supportive when I wrote a story in first grade about sentient pink clouds and it runner-upped in some bullshit competition—and they continue to be supportive to this day. Rita Pagenkopf suggested I become an English teacher perhaps one (thousand) too many times but only because she cared about me a lot. Thanks to Phil and Allison, Dana, Lauren, and Debbie for being family. Thanks to the residents of Witkem (Kyla Ernst-Alper, Molly Ernst-Alper, Mendel Rabinovitch, Austin Mitchell, Melissa Corning, and Alex Weinberg) for positive vibes. Thanks to my therapist, even though a distinct, lifelong lack of Lexapro created invaluable "research" for the topic at hand.

AUTHORS' NOTE

Hello, and thank you for making it to the inside part of our book! If you liked the words on the outside, you'll be dazzled by the sheer number of them to come. We hope you find it cozy and hospitable in here. After all, the world is a brutal place. Even if you, like us (Josh and Joe), have largely been exempt from life's most grisly horrors, your daily routine likely consists of onslaughts of unpleasantness punctuated by brief periods of relief, like a Pixies song. Also, if you're anything like us, lots of this discomfort is your own fault.

Wait! Don't go! We promise things get more fun! (Well, at least in the book. We can't vouch for the rest of your life.)

What we mean to say is, even if you have never served as a child soldier, found yourself unjustly imprisoned, or lost a loved one to a global pandemic, you *have* faced your own challenges. Every person's plight looks relatively tame next to somebody else's. Although if you've continued to play competitive tennis after losing a leg in a shark attack, you are definitely a better person than either of us.

Sometimes these obstacles to happiness are external. Perhaps you accidentally touched a pigeon with your bare hand or rode a bus next to a couple in the midst of a breakup. Much of our daily suffering, though, we bring upon ourselves. We show up to work hungover. We forget to call our parents on their birthdays. We spend embarrassing sums of money on cold-press juicers that we'll "totally use like every day." No one makes us do these things; they're mistakes we make over and over of our own free will. But it's not our fault. Or, to put it another way, it is. There is literally no one else to blame.

We (Joe and Josh) have written this book as a catalog of the ways we all make our lives harsher, broker, achier, sadder, angrier, smellier, more awkward, more embarrassing, and otherwise worse. For instance, have you ever had to convince your more successful acquaintances to write a blurb for your book cover? Not fun!

We hope that by reading this book, you will feel less like a failure (even if you recently lost your life savings trying to develop an app that's "like Facebook for pugs") and less alone (even if you live by yourself in a studio apartment in Kotzebue, Alaska). Please, join us as we stare deep into our souls, shake our heads, and vow to do whatever the soul equivalent of a million crunches is next year.

So lie back on your futon, fainting sofa, or whatever item of furniture you use for relaxation, and let our words massage away your shame. At least while you're reading, you can't screw anything else up. Unless you have somewhere to be. *Do* you have somewhere to be? What time is it? Eh. It's probably too late to make it even if you leave now.

Look at that. As always, you blew it!

FRIENDS, FAMILY, AND EVERYONE ELSE WHO DRIVES YOU CRAZY

———————

CHAPTER 1

Friends Like These

Every year after your twenty-second birthday, it becomes more difficult to make new friends. Nobody told you this when you were a child because you would've cried about it until given ice cream or a pony. As children, two people can form an intense bond over simply not being the kid who threw up on the monkey bars that time. Once we're old enough to file our own taxes, though, we've become conditioned to assume everyone we meet has enough friends already. As hard as it is to make new friends in adulthood, though, it's easier than ever to lose them.

Friendship dynamics evolve over time. In high school, half your friends hated each other and only stuck together because, well, what else were they gonna do—hang out at a cooler high school, where the principal spends most of his time with a small group of students at a nearby fifties-themed diner? Adults don't have to do that. Our busy lives both explain and excuse losing touch. All it takes now is one perceived slight, and we never text that buddy from urban kickball league ever again.

Of course, this disposability isn't true of old friends. Anyone whose wedding you were in won't kick you to the curb because you declined to "like" one of their Facebook status updates. (Although he or she probably will move to Scarsdale and breed, thus defriending you by natural causes.) It's the new people in your life you actually worry about. A blossoming adult friendship is a delicate soufflé under constant threat of collapsing under its own weight and turning into egg chum. But unlike the soufflé we destroyed back in home ec class, with friends you don't get credit just for showing up.

Making Plans and Breaking Plans

Even if much of friendship can now be literally phoned in, most of us still like to actually meet up from time to time and gaze at our phones together in person. Every year, though, it seems there are fewer hours in each day and more reasons not to leave the house. Spending time in the same room as your friends used to be an essential part of forging a community, and still is, but now you can get that same feeling of togetherness from protesting a sitcom cancellation while doing five other things and not wearing pants. If people meet up less than they once did, it's also because making plans has started to feel like a cold-war showdown of who will cancel first.

It's pretty much expected that before any two people meet up they will first cancel back and forth five or six times, like two awful ships in the night piloted by first-time ship captains. One part of the problem is scheduling. If you pick a date too soon, your friend probably can't make it; pick one too far out, and you come across like your own executive assistant trying to pencil someone in for a "deskside." Choosing a time frame *is* crucial, though, because everybody knows that "Let's meet up some-time" is code for "See you never."

Getting together and doing stuff always *sounds* like some-thing Future You would do. Future You is down for whatever. On the day of, though, Current You is more "down comforter," and doesn't want to go anywhere—which is often the optimal outcome. But bailing on friends too often puts you on that slip-pery slope toward becoming the Boy Who Cried RSVP. That's why there's a protocol for cancellation.

On the day you're supposed to meet with a friend, it's fairly standard to check in and confirm that neither of you has died nor had a conflicting appendectomy come up. Some people even offer an out during this check-in, a chance to reschedule if need be. Any mention of a rain check, though, is a self-fulfilling prophecy. Unless you're seriously *pumped* about after-work drinks, it seems almost rude to not reschedule when your friend offers. He or she probably just wanted to put this off until later but didn't want to be the jerk who pulled the trigger. It's like a vampire playing coy about needing to be invited in until you just give up and throw your neck blood right onto his fangs.

After canceling and rescheduling enough times, it's clear that this is all a charade and neither of you really wants to see the other. Actually meeting up at this point would be like listening to the decades-delayed Guns N' Roses album *Chinese Democracy*— confusing and unnecessary. Neither of you come right out and pronounce the plan over. Instead, you slowly starve it out, with-drawing from Gchats, avoiding all mention of this idea, until it withers and dies. When two weeks have gone by without men-tioning your coffee date, you've both officially won at cancel-chess. Congratulations, you're free.

I Don't Know Why You Say Good-bye, I Say Hello

If you're anything like us—and God help you if so—you're not out of the woods just because you do make time to see a friend. Assuming you're seeing this person on purpose, you may want to actually, you know, talk to her. Unfortunately, there are plenty of ways to botch both the entry and dismount of conversation.

The Handshake

What was once a simple clenching of fingers for the purpose of making sure the other person wasn't going to stab you with a sword is now a minefield of unregulated finger gymnastics.

First off, how much pressure do you apply during a hand-shake? You don't want to go too hard with it. You would seem psychotic. Squeezing an acquaintance's hand with a metric ton per square inch of pressure is like dunking over your seven-year-old nephew. You've just proved that you are a big strong person who has no restraint.

But you also don't want to leave your hand completely limp, like your limbs are made of uncooked steak. It's unnerving. Un-less you are a surgeon or someone else who does delicate, creepy work with their fingers, grip firmly. Don't be gross.

Even once you've gauged the appropriate pressure with which to clamp, there's still the issue of handshake style. Do you pump once? Twice? Thrice? (Answer: One pump is standard, two is for politicians, and three is reserved for characters played by Chris Farley in early 1990s *SNL* sketches.)

Plus, over the past few years, the handshake-shift-grip-pull-in-for-a-hug-and-backslap has become increasingly popular. That move says: "I want to hug you, but I'm worried things are moving too fast. Oops. It happened." Usually it's men doing this. Women often feel less shame about showing physical affection to their friends, whether it's hugging, cheek kisses, or making out while drunk and talking about it twice a year. On average, women are much less emotionally repressed.

The Fist Bump

A fist pound is a simple, no-frills greeting. Unfortunately, it has permeated the public consciousness to a point where everyone knows it, but nobody knows exactly when to do it. A fist bump sends one of several diverse messages. It could mean anything from . . .

"Thanks for coming to my fraternity mixer," to . . .

"I am a germophobe," but also . . .

"I just saw a movie about cool inner-city teens in the eighties," or . . .

"We're both wearing rings that when touched together give us superpowers!"

Worst of all, there's no way out of a fist bump if the other person rejects you. After a snubbed handshake, you can run the re-

buffed fingers through your hair. In this case, you're left holding a
lonesome fist in front of you with nowhere to put it. If this happens to you, simply punch yourself in the face and declare, "I'm
dumb!" It is no more awkward than what was already happening.

The Hug

Unless you're European, a full-on hug is the most intimate
form of friend greeting, except when you do it wrong. Hugging is
like lovemaking but with your clothes on, and you can do it with
people you're not attracted to even when you're sober and not
trying to get revenge on someone. (Who's living in the past NOW,
Rebecca?) What we mean to say is, it is a close-up smooshing of
bodies against one another that could go wrong at any moment,
especially if one person is more into it than the other.

When one person goes for a hug and the other person offers
only a handshake, it is a rejection as powerful as the "I love
you"..."I know" scene from *The Empire Strikes Back*. Even if a
hug does end up happening, it'll be a rigid, hips three feet apart,
room for the Holy Ghost hug. The kind you thought you left
behind when you stopped going to middle school dances.

Exit Through the Gift Shop

"Parting," as Shakespeare wrote, "is such sweet sorrow." But usually it's just the regular kind of sorrow, completely devoid of any
sugar or aspartame. Every departure presents the same pitfalls
as a greeting, plus a few more opportunities to show that you
barely know how to be a person.

Given what we've already mentioned about planning social events, the best way to say good-bye to a friend is to make direct eye contact, count to three in unison, and then shout: "LET'S TOTALLY DO THIS AGAIN SOON. I KNOW YOU'RE VERY BUSY, BUT I'LL TEXT YOU WHEN I HAVE A BETTER IDEA WHAT MY WEEK LOOKS LIKE." Then run in opposite directions, regardless of where you parked or what subway you need to take, and move to a new city.

This technique subverts the discomfort of both planning a future engagement and the multiple good-byes that occur when both people leave in the same direction. It always plays out the same way: The laughter at each false ending grows more strained. The shrugs get more cartoonish. This is why we recommend using the second half of any meet-up to draw a map of each person's exit strategy like you're planning a prison break. Color-code each individual route, if you have to. Anything's better than a series of exponentially more queasy iterations of "I guess *this* is good-bye for real" until one of you is finally inside an apartment.

Say It to My Facebook

When friends from separate circles meet in real life, you hope it's as cordial as a UN meeting. Not necessarily on social media, though. Friends of yours who will never meet in person might butt heads in the comments of your Facebook status, and rather than whipping these opposing factions into order, you hope they fight each other to the death like Colosseum gladiators. That's just one way interactions with friends online are much different than in person. All that remains is the constant threat of embarrassment.

Each strain of social media offers the same opportunity to validate your opinions and your lifestyle in general. It's officially confirmed that the double-gluten brownie you baked looks delicious. Everyone agrees that Sunday is indeed Funday. We crave affirmations like hamsters pressing buttons to get more pellets. (Pellets of heroin. In this scenario, you're a hamster involved in a heroin experiment.)

On the other hand, if you like every single status your friend writes, then, in true nihilist fashion, you like nothing. Some friends go the other way, though, never affirming anything you post online. Which is fine! Maybe he or she is busy, you know, *actually doing shit*. But now anytime you think about Jody, you're thinking about "Jody, who hates everything I say and wishes I was dead."

If your friends are ever mad at you, social media has made it easier than ever to find out, or delude yourself into that conclusion. It used to be a common fear that everyone is having a good time without you. Thanks to Twitter, Facebook, and Instagram, though, you can now see everybody hanging out without you in real time, all the time. On the bright side, not being invited to a heavily photographed event means you won't have to ask anybody to untag you from any pictures where it looks like you have a wonky eye. (All the pictures. All of them. What is wrong with your eye?)

Friends of Friends: The Strangers We Spend Time With

There's nothing better than spending time with old friends. You develop an intimacy and a shorthand that is enriched over time, a lack of pretense. Words that don't have any specific importance to the culture at large conjure cherished memories because of a mutually remembered goofy thing that happened one time.

That said, being forced to tag along with friends of friends and witness other people's inside jokes is a *Clockwork Orange*-esque immersion into horror. That exact same type of shorthand that brings so much joy among friends—only between *other* friends—looks to you like the demented scrawling of a madman.

What really makes friends of friends worse than outright strangers is that you're expected to get along with them. At a party full of randos, you can be honest. You can argue. You can ignore the folks you don't care for. But when you're connected by a mutual acquaintance, you're supposed to behave nicely, like you're on a playdate set up by your parents.

Going your whole life without having at least a minor dustup with a FOAF (Friend of a Friend) is impossible, because most of your friends' friends are assholes. In fact, most of your friends are probably assholes, too; it's just that you've learned to love them. Statistically, you're probably an asshole. We don't have the numbers on hand, but trust us. It's true.

That's why it's so stressful when separate groups of your friends meet. Any gathering where most of the attendees don't know each other is like a dog park for humans. And dogs at a dog park don't get along. They posture. They yap. They pee on things. These dangers apply to people as well, although humans are generally more adept at taking commands like: "Hey, get that out of your mouth!" and "Let's not talk about Israel, okay?"

It's a situation that can't be remedied. Every generally good person is someone else's asshole, as illustrated previously. That's

why every FOAF meeting has trailer-park meth-lab explosion
potential. To you, your friends are just your friends. You love
them all. But what if you accidentally invite Borderline Racist
Friend to dinner with Gets Offended by Every Single Thing
Friend? You're in for a long night of "I don't think that's what
Gary meant by 'those people.' Please stop shouting Maya Ange-
lou poetry in this restaurant." Just as disastrous can be pairing
Unambitious Hometown Friend with Pretentious Globe-trotter
Friend. "Actually, it's pronounced *phuh*. It's a Vietnamese noodle
soup." Relax, buddy. Nobody doubts that you backpacked in Asia
after junior year. You don't have to overenunciate every single
teriyaki dish and martial art for the rest of your life to prove it.

Sinking Friendships: Acquaintances to Avoid

We have lots of otherwise great friends whose worst qualities are amplified in unfamiliar settings. Combining any of
those ingredients, which can be wonderful on their own,
will lead to a foul-tasting hobo chili of camaraderie. So be
careful whom you bring into contact with one another or
your two favorite people could become mortal enemies.
Like these people:

- Cries After Two Drinks Friend

- Loves Strip Clubs Friend

- Suddenly Got Really Religious Friend

- Can't Get Over Their Ex Friend

- Won't Leave Their Own Neighborhood Friend

- Plays in a Shitty Band Friend

- Can't Do *Anything* Without Their Significant Other Friend
- Never Carries Cash Friend
- Comes from Money Friend
- Used to Be Poor and Is Now a Rich Dick Friend

If You Can't Say Something Nice, You'll Probably Still Say It

Most people are horrendous when it comes to accepting compliments. Offer the slightest praise about, say, their performance in a play, and they vehemently deny it as though you asked if they'd ever had a sexy dream about you. As annoying as this behavior is, and as awkward as it can get when a friend fishes for compliments and you don't take the bait, sometimes it's the person doling out the praise who can turn a celebratory moment into a fiasco. Some compliments are barely better than saying nothing at all, but others are worse than if you had said nothing while giving a double thumbs-down and shaking your head slowly.

Hate, Actually

The word "actually" conveys surprise where none should be, and can therefore be taken as an insult. Saying your friend is *actually* good at basketball means you're amazed that he is able to overcome the insurmountable obstacles set by his height and Judaism.

Paparazzi-ing

Even if the celebrity you think your friend looks like is objectively attractive, making the comparison out loud is bound to backfire. There's every chance you'll accidentally bring up the celebrity your friend hates or, more interesting, the celebrity who hates your friend.

The Non-pliment

Here is a short list of things that are fascinating: serial killers, stunt bartending, David Lynch movies, and the healing of scars. If you call your friend's appearance or creative output "interesting," you're *actually* pretty good at being kind of a dick. Compliments without any value judgment are just observations. Saying "Oh, you got a haircut!" instead of "Nice haircut!" makes you sound like a toddler excited about learning new words.

Unimprovement

Telling someone he "cleans up nicely" means the rest of the calendar year he dresses like a Dickensian chimney sweep. If you're too emphatic about how great your friend looks now, he gets embarrassed about how he looked before—like when you go see your barber and he gives you a look that says, "How have you even been walking around like this?"

The Investigator

"How are you still single?" isn't flattering praise—it's an invitation to categorize your most private flaws for the sake of small talk.

The False Idol

Almost anything you tell your friend she is "brave" for doing is something you would not be caught dead doing yourself. You don't really wish you were "confident enough to wear that dress." You just know you would *confidently* throw that dress in the trash if given the chance.

Known Unknowns

Knowledge is power. Take something as simple as a person's name. If you don't remember the name of an acquaintance, it's totally fine. In the average week, we interact with approximately one hundred Arcade Fires' worth of people and they're not all gonna stick. What's unacceptable is guessing someone's name. You're definitely not going to get it right. Even worse is forgetting the name of a friend's significant other. Now there are two people mad at you. Not remembering at all, though, is much preferable to calling that friend's current significant other the name of his or her ex. Doing so might break up their relationship and give you the reputation of a reverse matchmaker. Chickenshits everywhere will seek you out to break up their relationships for them. Remembering people's names is super important—and if you remember the names of their dogs, too, you deserve a human treat.

On the other hand, sometimes pretending *not* to know stuff makes conversations go smoother.

Interrupt your friend's soul-bearing moment to mention that Vanessa already gave you the gist, and now you're spending ten minutes discussing how Vanessa is the worst. (Of course, Vanessa and your friend will also have this discussion later about you. Everybody in your circle of friends is equi-worst.)

When you're not pretending to know information or pretending to not know it, you might be giving something away you're not supposed to. It could be a secret—or more likely something you didn't realize was a secret until it's too late. This is why you are never to speak of parties you've been invited to until you are actually there at the party, completely covered in nacho crumbs and margarita salt. Way more people are not invited to any given party than are invited, and anyone you mention a party to definitely wasn't yet aware this party exists. It stings a lot less to find out a party happened and you weren't invited than to know a party's about to happen and everyone's going but you. Not that we have any idea what that's like. If you ever don't see us at a party, it's because we had a cooler party to go to. Beyoncé was probably performing there. But we were totally invited. Trust us.

CHAPTER 2

Awful in the Family

Your family is like an Aerosmith song: It was around before you got here, it's never going away, and there's a good chance it's going to feature some overwrought shrieking and tense father-daughter interplay. The kicker is, even if your relatives are all as unpleasant as the average set of *Real World/Road Rules* challengers, they still (hopefully) kept you from being eaten by wolves as a baby. A family reunion is, at the most basic level, a celebration of an entire group of people who, over the course of generations, did not let anyone get eaten by wolves. (If someone had, they certainly would not be welcome at Aunt Linda's place on the Cape.)

The family dynamic is as delicate and dangerous as a spiderweb. Chances are, you've either gotten perilously snared in yours or have swept it away entirely with the bristly broom of "going to art school" or "marrying a third-tier porn star named the Gooch." So really, a family is more like a snowflake: unique

but easily destroyed. There are nearly as many awesome meta-
phors for families as there are families.

Siblinguistics

Your sibling can be your best friend or your worst enemy. Maybe
you'll luck out with a "cool" older sister who exposes you to
good music and teaches you which alcoholic beverages Mom
and Dad won't be able to smell on your breath. Maybe you get to
be the hip older brother. But be careful. The uncool sibling who
thinks he or she is cool is the worst kind of relative. If you've
ever said, "Guys love a girl who can do celebrity impressions" or
"Learn all the words to this Steely Dan album, and you can sit at
whatever lunch table you want," you are not a cool older sibling.
You're just a weirdo whose parents have had sex at least twice.

What you don't want is a sibling who is too successful. You'll
look bad in comparison. But neither do you want one who's a
total loser. He'll always be asking you for money or for you to hit
him with your car as part of an insurance scam. If you're doing
better financially than your brother or sister, it's awkward when
you come home for the holidays (she doesn't need to come
home; she still lives there). You look like a jerk and a show-off
bringing an expensive bottle of wine when your younger brother
can only afford to give family members handwritten massage
coupons and half-used Dunkin' Donuts gift cards as birthday
presents.

Parents: They Brought You Into This World, and Sometimes They Make You Want to Leave It.

Unless you're Batman, you probably grew up with at least one parent. (And if you are Batman, thanks for reading our book. We think you're pretty neat.) Everyone's relationship with his or her parents is different. It can range from "we don't talk," which is sad, to "my parents are my best friends," which is, well, sadder. The bond between parents and children is strong. After all, your parents are the only humans you've ever lived inside. Although, to be fair, you were very, very small when you were inside your father's body, and there's a good chance you don't remember much of it.

A healthy relationship with one's parents requires constant vigilance, and the easiest way for you to facilitate its destruction is to simply ignore it. Most parents like to "check in" with their children fairly frequently. Checking in usually takes place on speakerphone. In fact, it is the *only* thing that usually takes place on speakerphone other than conference calls, which are somehow less productive than talking to your parents. The purpose of checking in is to make sure you are not dead. Parents spend a significant portion of their income raising their children, and if those kids just go off and *die*, the return on investment (ROI) looks pathetic.

In our experience, parents spend most of their days inventing creative scenarios in which their children have died. *Are you out to dinner and not checking your voice mail? Perhaps you choked to death in the bathroom. That's where most people do that, you know. They're embarrassed to ask for help and they never learned to self-*

Heimlich, despite someone *suggesting it so many times. Don't be like that. Your mother is worried about you.*

Missing a call from your parents will set off a phone tree of desperation like the one the government uses in the event of a nuclear threat. If you don't pick up the phone when your parents call, their brains write an entire season of *Law & Order: SVU* about you until you get back to them. Although, remember, once you take the call, it will be nearly impossible to hang up. Parents cling to the phone lines like glitter sticks to human skin. A subtle "anyway . . ." or "I should let you go" normally doesn't suffice. To be sure you make a clean exit, shout, "I said good day, sir!" and hang up emphatically.

Other reasons for a check-in include inquiring whether you are any closer to becoming wealthy or married than you were the previous week. It's important to parents that you're wealthy or married (unless they're dedicated hippies, in which case it's crucial to them that you avoid wealth and find a partner who makes your moonbeam shine brightly, or some such thing). A "wealthy" status is important because of the aforementioned financial investment in your upbringing. A "married" status mostly gives them something to talk about with their friends and members of your extended family of whom you yourself are only dimly aware.

If you are not yet wealthy, your parents will worry, as well they should. Their generation is using up our nation's natural and financial resources at an unsustainable rate. Young people need to start saving money in the womb so that they'll be able to pay off their student debt and put some cash away for retirement or for jettisoning themselves into space in hopes of landing on a planet that still has potable drinking water and breathable air.

Back here on Earth, though, having a job is different than having a career. Whether you assess insurance risks or sell dream catchers made from your body hair on Etsy, one thing is for certain: Your parents will not understand your life's work. They will ask you the same questions over and over. Or, they will ask a series of questions that do not actually pertain to your life. ("So, how many chemical compounds have you invented?" "I teach high school science, Mom.") Often, they'll do both, especially if you are pursuing a career in "the arts." The only way to have a career that your parents understand is to be able to afford health insurance out of pocket. If you can do that, your parents will acknowledge you could have survived when they were growing up, before people started "following their dreams" and "letting women have jobs, too." Making a decent wage shows your parents that you are no longer a toddler, and if you get eaten by a wolf now, it's your own damn fault.

If you do manage to make a lot of money, congratulations... that must be nice. We're super psyched for you. You don't need to call your parents and pretend to be interested in the shady politics of their bridge league, looking for a proper segue to ask them about PayPalling you rent money. But there are still other problems to contend with. When you go out to dinner with your parents, do you offer to pay? Will that make them proud of your independence or instill in them a keen awareness of your adulthood and by extension their own mortality? What about gifts? Do you expect them on birthdays anymore? Do you still have to pretend you like the socks they bought you? You have a job. If you wanted socks, you'd buy your own damn socks.

And what do you get *them*? A small, thoughtful token? (Note:

After age ten, a macaroni necklace doesn't cut it as a gift anymore.) Or do you make a big purchase to show that you wear big
boy (or girl) pants now? Either way, it's impossible to find a present so impressive it makes up for all the crying and pooping you
did from birth to age twenty-one. Don't worry. Where your parents are concerned, any issue of money can be weird as long as
you live. Unlike your mushroom cut and JNCO jeans in high
school, this does not get better.

One thing that never changes, though, is that parents like to
tell their children anything that happens to them. They'll gladly
share the minutest of minutiae with you. Did your dad run into
the parent of someone you once played youth soccer against? Prepare to hear about it! Did they have an unsatisfying experience
with a bank teller? *Buckle up! You're in for a tale!* You have to listen
because, again, they didn't feed you to alligators when you were a
teenager.

It's also crucial *how* you listen, though. The two most important tasks are mustering interest in their every observation and
remembering which scandalous facts about other family members are secrets not to be brought up with any outsiders you may
be sleeping with. All this would be simpler to keep track of if the
line between public and private hadn't grown blurrier than a
three A.M. bar light over the past ten years.

So Your Mom's on Facebook

Remember the halcyon days of the 1990s, when your parent had
to actually show up in person to embarrass you? Well, that's no
longer the case.

As social media has become less of a way for college kids to waste time and more of a way for actual adults to waste time, our elders have started dipping their toes into the pool, too. And Facebook, of course, is the shallow end: full of pictures and positive affirmations, and allowing the ability to leave long-winded comments with minimal self-awareness. If one of your parents has sent you a Facebook friend request, it's already too late. Your best course of action is to let it go and pretend you never saw it, hoping they don't really understand how Facebook works (not unlikely) or that the subject never comes up (highly unlikely).

If you thought getting chain e-mails full of urban legends with subject lines like: "Fw: Fw: Fw: Fw: Fw: Fw: Obamascare" was annoying, it turns out that's just the beginning. A parent who runs amok on social media can complicate/worsen your life in many different ways. Regardless of one's age, level of physical fitness, and gender identity, a parent leaving the comment "gorgeous" or, even worse, "hawt" on any and/or every Facebook/Instagram picture is an incredibly effective cock block (or, for women, a "vajector seat"). Similarly, a mother or father who overpraises your achievements on social media reduces the dignity of your career to high school talent show level. You got a promotion, but you're being celebrated like you wheezed your way through a sweaty, pitchy rendition of "Castle on a Cloud" from *Les Misérables*.

The most mortifying parental sin on social media, however, is when a parent interacts with your friends, coworkers, or nemeses online. It's one thing for your mother to write "my Angel!" on a picture of you at a barbecue taken immediately before you passed out drunk in a plate of ribs. It's another thing entirely for her to write "Happy birthday!" on the timeline of your high school crush whom you slept with at your five-year reunion and haven't talked to since.

The only upside to having your parents on social media is that they will usually feel up-to-date on your life and will have fewer questions when they see you in person or talk to you on the phone. This one minor boon, however, is often outweighed by the number of Internet acronyms you'll have to explain to them. (Side note: Lying about these things doesn't help. If you tell your dad that FML means "Finding My Love," you can guarantee within an hour he'll post something like, "Looking for my darling wife in the living room. FML.")

Everything's Relatives

The good news is, your extended family is hard to disappoint. The bad news is, that's because they don't care very much about you one way or the other. Even if you're a total screwup, you're not a disappointment; you're more like a circus sideshow. Every family needs a Lobster Boy.

For some people, cousins are close friends. For most, however, they're acquaintances whose names are hard to keep straight. Anybody further from you than a first cousin shares the same amount of DNA with you as a gorilla, basically. If you like them at all, you've won the genetic jackpot. Your prize, however, is just slightly less awkwardness at weddings.

Grandparents are the hardest to let down. They love you unconditionally. You're basically the reason they made your parents. So you have that going for you. The only thing you can do to upset a grandparent is not be married, or marry the wrong person, or be married for more than fifteen minutes without having kids, or not be a doctor, or be the wrong kind of doctor, or be a doctor but not also a lawyer, or be a doctor and a lawyer but not have a nice car, or be a doctor and a lawyer who drives a nice car but doesn't volunteer, or not call often enough. So, pretty much, there's nothing you can do to upset a grandparent.

In-laws: The Other Significant Others

The most fragile relationship you'll ever face is the twist tie that binds you to your significant other's family. It's a link that is only as strong as you and your partner's love for one another. Actually, it's not even that powerful. It's only really as solid as your partner's love for you. Because if your partner changes her mind, but you keep loving her, the family will likely take her side and file a restraining order no matter how pure your intentions, and cross you off the holiday card list as well.

Your significant other's parents are especially tricky. They're family in the way that guests at Olive Garden are family. You want them to like you so they don't tear your relationship apart with an emergency intervention (aka a "shotgun divorce"), but your very existence is a burden to them. A quick checklist of ways to upset the temperamental ecosystem of this dynamic:

- Act too familiar. "Hey, Papa Smurf! How's it hanging?"
- Be not friendly enough. Sitting silently at dinner like a serial killer plotting his or her next move is terrifying, not respectful.

- Mention specific sex things you've done with your current partner.
- Imply you've ever done sex things with a previous partner.
- Show up to a family gathering empty-handed.
- Never show up to family gatherings.
- Like the wrong sports team.
- Like sports *too* much.
- Not like sports at all.
- Be the wrong religion.
- Be the right religion, but in the wrong way.
- Vote with your heart.
- Vote with your wallet.
- Curse like a sailor.
- Drink like a sailor.
- Sail.

Kids: A Brand-new You

If your existing family sits on *too* rock-solid a foundation, you should consider having children. It's always easier to ruin something when you get in on the ground floor, and a child is nearly impossible not to mess up. If you want to screw an adult up, you have to go far out of your way. With a child, it's easy. Their squishy little brains are still learning how the world works, so they're ripe for tampering.

Children are gullible. You can lie to them about anything. Tell them yogurt is ice cream until they figure out what's really going on. Not only will you deprive them of ice cream, you'll also erode their ability to trust. It's really that easy! Give them an era-inappropriate name like Lazarus or Borptron3000. Tell them the tooth fairy is real until they're fourteen and then punish them for contradicting you. The possibilities are endless!

We've gotten this far without stating the obvious: Having a kid can ruin *your* life, too. Say good-bye to your free time, disposable income, friendships, ability to travel, sleep schedule, and sex life. You have a new full-time job, and that job is not just keeping an infant alive until it's an adult, but also making sure it doesn't become the kind of adult who wears sunglasses inside or uses the word "irregardless." Good luck!

Plus, having children will really showcase how much other people can love someone who isn't you. If you thought everyone else in your life cared about you, wait until you see how much they love your offspring. You'll feel like a real piece of garbage watching your supposed "loved ones" coo and fawn over a little bag of drool who can't even parallel park. Not to mention, no matter what you do, everyone in your life will question your every parenting decision, whether they've raised a child or not. Prepare to hear every criticism from: "Oh, you let them have refined sugar?" to "You've got to spank 'em hard and often. Otherwise, they get MFAs in poetry."

Yes, if you're hoping to really destroy several lives in one go, you can hardly do better than having a child.

CHAPTER 3

Roommates: The Leased Common Denominators

It's impossible to truly know a person until you've lived together. Pulitzer Prize–winning biographer Walter Isaacson, for example, spent years interviewing Steve Jobs and still found out less about him than he would've after a single bedbug scare or Time Warner Cable dispute. Jobs's official biography is woefully inadequate as a result, and now none of us will ever know the real him. Thanks for nothing, Isaacson!

You might think you know everything about your friends and relatives and whomever it is you're sleeping with, but that's just you being delusional. You should stop being so delusional all the time. Here's the thing: Your friends are gross, your relatives are disgusting, and your boyfriend or girlfriend belongs in a zoo—maybe even one of those superzoos, with cages that self-clean like produce aisles with sprinklers. But it's totally fine, because guess what—you're gross, too! We all are! Thankfully, nobody knows just *how* gross anyone else is until they move in together. That's what true love is: two consenting adults who discover just how horrific each is, and don't mind. But first, most people end up finding out way too much about a rotating freak show of roommates.

People can start almost anywhere on the stranger-to-friend spectrum of roommates, but unlike young couples living together, there's no chance of these relationships blossoming into something more. Friends will not become best friends, and barely tolerated Craigslisters won't become buddies. The best that most of us can hope for is just coming out on the other side free of litigation and future blackmail attempts. Beyond dirty dishes and late rent, roommates must often deal with plenty of other quietly crushing situations that even Steve Jobs couldn't help to prevent. Or maybe he could've! That's something we'll never know. Because Walter Isaacson is very bad at his job.

How to Blow It in Every Room of Your House

When shared houses devolve into landfills of anxiety, it's often because of tensions specific to each room. Let's take a tour of a typical home to see where the problems are. Unlike with the tours your friends offer of their new homes, we won't get mad if you decline. (Just kidding; it'd mean a lot to us if you read this chapter. What can we do to make that happen? We have kettle corn....)

Kitchen

If you live with just one person, congratulations—you'll never have to go all *Magnum, P.I.* over some missing baba ghanoush. Knowing where your food went doesn't make confronting someone about it any easier, though. You still have to act like a paranoid food monitor, surveying changes to the fridge's contents with clinical interest. Having a stolen food conversation is the first step toward padlocked mini-fridges, nanny cams, and someone actively embezzling salsa just to get inside your head. So it had better be worth it.

Preparing food is no picnic either. Well, unless you're preparing food for a picnic, in which case, can we come? With roommates, one will be cooking dinner when another comes in wanting to do the very same thing. Sure, two people can cook in a cramped space at the same time, but this requires a soupçon of steely politeness as you force each other to scoot around one tiny kitchen. Whoever was there first wonders why the second person couldn't just wait, and the second person is upset the first was ever born. Any tepid conversation that bubbles up is almost always about how hungry each of you is, as if the more ravenous person has the more legit grievance. You'll talk about almost anything except what's really on both of your minds, which is, "Oh my god, why are you even here? Not just in this kitchen, but this planet in general."

If the space truly is too small for two people to cook, the second person might still stick around and wait in the kitchen. For some people, this is torture. When cooking by yourself, you can do whatever you want, like drinking spaghetti sauce straight from the jar without fear of reprisal. However, when someone is watching you prepare food, you have to act as if you were auditioning for the role of a chef in a movie or reality TV series. Explaining that you'd prefer to cook alone, though, sounds like the ruse of someone who is in the midst of hunting for treasure buried in the walls of the kitchen. Now you're just two hungry pals being annoyed around food together.

Bathroom

Much like its spiritual opposite, the kitchen, the bathroom is in constant demand from all roommates at all times. Mornings are especially hectic, because most of us wait to shower until the last possible moment—which usually ends up being the moment someone else decides to take a lights-out sadness bath with lavender-scented votive candles.

The only way to ever get in there first is to develop a nascent awareness of the floor creaks that indicate someone is about to beat you to the punch, like how French-Canadian trappers sense a creature rustling in the forest before they even hear it. Then you might find yourself pirouetting into the bathroom at the sound of a turned doorknob on the other side of the house. Anything to win.

If you actually make it in time, all you have to deal with is your roommate's exasperated sigh and probably some residual tension the next time you encounter each other. If you don't get there first, however, you'll both be standing next to the bathroom door with equal claim to it, each wishing the other had some sort of injury requiring a catheter. Ask to go first and your wish will likely be granted. A poo-related emergency, though, trumps a shower crisis, and if the latter is yours, you have to stand down. Either way, the whole exchange feels like it's enveloped in a dense fog bank of lumberjack BO (because it stinks).

Most people would prefer not to let anyone know they have a functional digestive system at all. We spend our lives slinking in and out of a series of bathrooms, hopefully unnoticed. When your roommate heads in right after you, though, it puts you in the mortifying position of having to say, "Hey, you probably should wait a couple of minutes—I just fucking *destroyed* the bathroom." It feels mutually invasive, like someone has been forced to join in a human centipede with you. Even though it's way better to be the head of a centipede than next in line, you still feel embarrassed for that person.

Hallways

It doesn't take especially refined taste to know somebody else has terrible taste. You could be a minimalist with a low budget and no ideas and still deem a roommate's poster of dueling female dragons unacceptable. Although the living room is the "big dance" of home decorations, your hallways are also representative of your outlook on life. As such, they should probably not feature any hentai tentacle porn. Unfortunately, telling someone he has awful taste is like telling him that his tattoo sucks—you're probably right, but who died and made you editor of *Tattoo Judge Magazine*?

Since taste is subjective, your argument is unwinnable. You might end up still having to look at the wall trash in question every day, with your opinions on it now out in the open. Either that or you could fake a break-in. Surely there are cat burglars attracted to objectionable art.

Living Room

Sometimes the worst thing a roommate can do to a living room is occupy it. If the same person is always there, slathered across the couch like an old ketchup stain, you will come to hate this person. You will listen at the door for traces of *The Big Bang Theory* when you come home, feel your heart flare up with hatred when you do, and brace for the joyless exchange to come. Unfortunately, you can't just flat-out ask someone to not be somewhere all the time. You can try a revenge occupation, to give the other person a taste of his or her own medicine. This plan will probably backfire, though, with your roommate plopping down right next to you, lifestyle validated.

Bedroom

Unless you live inside the soundproof confines of a *Hustle & Flow*–style home recording studio, anyone you share a wall with leaves large audio footprints. The two of you are starring in the most boring radio play of all times—and both pretending you can't hear it. There is an unspoken agreement among roommates that anything happening behind closed doors is a total mystery. So when one of you acknowledges hearing anything through the walls, it shatters the delicate illusion that there *isn't* another human sleeping eighteen inches away (like at summer camp or an orphanage).

It doesn't even have to be an obvious betrayal, like high-fiving your roommate for ending a six-month sexual dry spell. ("I've never heard a human being so grateful for physical contact before," you might say, pushing a Popsicle through a bagel for effect.) All it takes to make somebody uncomfortable is mentioning that you heard him absently singing along to Meghan Trainor, or having an extensive self–pep talk. It's like finding out your room has been wiretapped. You become more guarded, like Jim Carrey finding out his whole life is on TV in *The Truman Show*, and it's even more disappointing than most of the things he's done since that movie.

Passive-Aggressive Notes, or "It's the Notes You Don't Say"

Of all the ways to establish boundaries, the only one worse than shivving your roommate with a sharpened toothbrush is leaving a passive-aggressive note. Whenever off-limits food gets eaten or Tupperwared leftovers sprout biology, certain folks feel the need to vent their spleen remotely, and on paper. Big mistake! An aggrieved note almost always makes matters worse— wrapping the typical awkward tension inside a deeper level of discomfort and essentially creating an awkwardness turducken.

Passive-aggressive notes are the best examples of a situation in which you can be in the right and handle it so wrong that it doesn't matter. Reading these notes is like peering into people's dreams: Their desires are visible, but so are the most unhinged aspects of their personality. It's clear that Gary would like to keep chunky salsa in the fridge without it slowly being pilfered away into just one sad little sliver of a serving, but it's also clear that Gary has fantasized about poisoning his own leftovers just to see which roommate takes ill.

If you Google "passive-aggressive note," you will find a bustling digital post office of handwritten notes that attempt humor while also being flagrantly mean. These people took the nuclear option, choosing to ruin any chance of living amicably. Passive-aggressive notes don't have to be Internet-worthy in order to backfire, though—just really smug and misguided. In fact, you may have even written such a note and not realized it. Try filling out the passive-aggressive note Mad Lib below to see if it resembles any of your greatest hits.

Passive-Aggressive Note Mad Libs

[too friendly greeting] [roommate you clearly hate],

　　We have to talk. You probably don't mean to [minor thing] on purpose, but [minor thing] keeps happening. I can see how if it were just once or twice, it wouldn't be that big a deal, but it's happened [triple actual number] times. Now I know we can sometimes forget we're supposed to not [minor thing]. Hell, even I from time to time have been known to [similar thing, but even more minor, somehow]. When we do it all the time, though, [dramatic description of inconvenience]. I know we're all busy with [condescending description of roommate's job], and that's fine. But rather than [dramatic consequence], I hope in the future we can please stop [what roommate almost always does] so that we can avoid [not even barely veiled threat].

　　　　　　　　　　　　　[too positive sign-off],

　　　　　　　　　　　　　[uptight a-hole (you)]

The Worst Roommates in the World

Could God make a roommate so unbearable even he couldn't stand to live with him or her? If so, it'd be one of these five people: the worst roommates there are.

The Borrower

When you know someone else is going to see your room, you tend to clean it to an inhabitable level of toxicity. Not so, the rest of the time. If nobody's coming over, most people follow the cleanliness path of least resistance, which translates to recently worn outfits flung on every surface like water in the Splash Zone at SeaWorld. That's why it sucks to think of the Borrower entering your room when you're not in it—even besides the fact that obviously he shouldn't be borrowing stuff without asking. Knowing that someone unauthorized has seen what your room looks like in its natural state feels like a violation on the level of demonic possession.

The Martyr

You'll always be aware when a Martyr comes home, thanks to the Greek chorus of world-weary sighs from another room (a room you will likely have vacated specifically to avoid this person). Any conversation you have with the Martyr will center on how busy he or she is, or the details of a thing about the house that is not perfect, and somehow it's always *your* fault.

The Pickup Artist

Before coming on to *anybody*, it's best to know the attraction is reciprocal. When it comes to a roommate, though, you pretty much need to have it in writing and then go to the bank and find a notary public to authorize this hookup. On the other hand, some bridge trolls will throw caution to the lease and hit on you or your friends based on a horny hunch. It is impossible to describe the difficulty of eating Frosted Flakes every day across from someone whose sexual advances you've rebuffed. It could be worse, though: The Pickup Artist could turn his attention to a neighbor; in which case, say hello to your unofficial new bonus roommate. The only benefit is that when the inevitable breakup happens, your roommate will move out and your neighbor will avoid you and they'll both be gone forever.

The Absentminded Professor

An absentminded roommate is not necessarily unintelligent, but he or she *will* do things you literally cannot believe. The negligence might involve safety—like leaving the front door wide open all day or the oven burners on all night. Or it might be based in hygiene—like leaving a toilet bowl filled with remnants of a pubic hair bonsai session, a ritualistic offering to the mythic king of male beauty, Testosteros. Whichever way the Absentminded Professor strikes, the result is the same—a conversation that grown adults should never have to have with each other. By the time you find yourself engaged in multiple interventions about this roommate's behavior, you won't be able to look him in the eye without wondering by which Darwinian loophole he's managed to survive this long.

Dr. Don'tlittle

Pets are awesome. They make great baby practice for couples considering kids, and they keep people who work from home sane, against overwhelming odds. However, some people desire all the benefits of having a pet without any of the responsibilities— and living with these people is, literally, super shitty. Looking after an animal that isn't yours, or convincing someone else to do a better job of it, will quickly foment revolution in an otherwise happy house. There's no good way to break the news to someone that she's not fit to be a pet owner. Especially when that person will, in turn, probably accuse you of just not being a dog person, which in the United States is considered almost worse than being a sex trafficker.

The Great Escape: Getting Out of a Roommate Situation

When it's time for you and a roommate to part ways, you can't mince words. Mincing words is for jackasses. No notes or e-mails, unless the situation is such that you are scared for your safety, in which case you're probably living in a mid-1990s erotic thriller (say hi to Gabriel Byrne for us!). Once you and your roommate have agreed to a platonic divorce, you might think you'd be impervious to any residual dis-ease going forward, but that is not the case. You must both endure the purgatory of the notification period leading up to the kick-out, and it's like living

with your ex right after a breakup. You'll fail at avoiding each
other just about every day, and as boring as small talk can be, the
acute lack of it between people who've fully given up on each
other is even more tense.

It's also not the time to finally say what you think about this
person. That's like asking out your class crush on the last day of
school because you won't see her again—only the opposite. This
person already knows you can't stand living with him, and the
rest of what you think you want to say is just details. Further-
more, pulling at this thread will unravel the entire sweater of
what human beings don't tell each other about each other. Your
roommate's turn will be next, and then you'll finally hear about
all the blind spots that make you a bad roommate/person, the
stuff you always feared. You'll finally see yourself, warts and all,
and be shocked by such a high concentration of warts.

Joe Blew It: Moving In Is Not a Piece of Cake

Random roommates always surprise you, but it's never a happy
surprise. It's usually more like the surprise of mildew on your
clothes or a subway that's not coming or Beck being a Scientolo-
gist. Sure enough, I spent most of my college years sharing
apartments with a rogue's gallery of subhumans. My senior year
was different, though. That's when I moved in with three actual
friends. It was an arrangement I'd been dreaming of since I'd first
learned college was even a thing—and one I would end up
wrecking almost immediately, the very day we moved in.

After several hours of U-Haul runs, all four of us were
tapped out. Tomorrow, we decided, would be the day for put-

ting stuff away and figuring out which *Reservoir Dogs* poster went where. In the meantime, we would celebrate our successful transfer of underpants and textbooks from three crappy, over-priced apartments into one crappy, overpriced apartment. We toasted our new shared residence, many times over, by doing shots—the style of drinking that most closely resembles shoot-ing oneself in the face.

We were still destroying our young, stupid livers a couple of hours later, when I was struck by the twin lightning bolts of in-spiration and that one vodka too many. You know, that special drink that helps you temporarily cross over into the spirit world. The following things then happened in the following order: I yelled "Oh, snap!" and ran down the hall to my room, I cranked up the volume on the new LP by Cake and hit REPEAT, and then I locked my door and dove into the warm embrace of slumber like a rail-riding vagabond safely stowed away in a cozy caboose.

Perhaps you're unfamiliar with the music of Cake. It kind of sounds like a bluegrass band engaged in a street brawl with ma-riachis, while an NPR announcer narrates everything. Cake is known for its monotonous front man and for keeping a full-time trumpeter on the payroll. In other words, kind of an acquired taste. Or so I found out.

I awoke the next morning in an apartment whose core tem-perature had radically changed overnight. The first obvious dif-ference was that there was now a constellation of scuff marks on the outside of my door, as though six angry feet had applied field goal–kicking strength to the task of making sure "Short Skirt/Long Jacket" didn't play one more time. The next big change was that everybody was crazy pissed at me, and not in the playful way of when a bro spills a beer on another bro. They were mad on a "reevaluating recent residential decisions" level. It turned out nobody had succeeded in waking me up and getting me to shut off the music. Apparently, I'd shut it off on my own at some point in the night, but not before my roommates had angrily trod off to their bedrooms and put in earbuds to escape the audio Möbius strip of Cake.

For the next several weeks, nobody in the house looked happy to see me. They didn't even look up from *Madden* on PlayStation to say hi as I shuffled by. I eagerly awaited the moment we'd look back on what had happened and laugh, but it never arrived. The Cake situation turned out to be something you just didn't bring up. It was a bad omen, but perhaps it was for the best. By the time we all started getting on each other's nerves regularly, a high-water mark had already been established, putting most grievances in flattering perspective. To this day, though, hearing the twang-funk of Cake always makes me imagine the batter of college friendship baking in an oven for far too long and setting off a smoke alarm that's impossible to shut off.

CHAPTER 4

Party Downers

When adults use the word "party" as a verb, sadly they're never talking about bouncy castles, close-up magic, or any other classic party ingredients. Instead, it usually just means getting fugue-state wasted in any setting at all. A squatting hermit, for instance, could spend the saddest evening imaginable sniffing glue in a dimly lit crawl space and be said to have partied pretty hard. Using the term this way is fitting, though, since parties are indeed highly intoxicating but also scary and terrible.

The slick surface of the parties glimpsed in movies and the entire discography of Pitbull is not as it appears. It's actually littered with anxiety land mines that can detonate whether stepped on by you or by an almost complete stranger with whom you can't seem to end a conversation. (Ideally, you should be able to say, "I'm done with you," and walk away—and, technically, you can—but then you'll still see this person again later and feel like a deadbeat dad confronted by the child he left behind.)

The danger begins immediately. You walk in and an entire room might introduce itself at once, everyone reciting their names like the *Sound of Music* kids, even though you've forgotten these names before they even hit your ear canal. Either that or you find you're the first to arrive—an eyewitness to the slow, gradual birthing process, which can be as painful for the observer as walking into an actual delivery room right on time. And that's just the beginning! There's an entire party left to foul, and, unlike Las Vegas, what happens at a party not only doesn't stay there, it echoes for an eternity. (Actually, the same goes for what happens in Vegas. That expression is horseshit.)

Work Parties

What is it?

Going to an office party can be like getting drafted into a long-form improv scene that goes on forever and alienates the audience. Everyone is trying to act like they've shown up of their own free will, and they do not quite have this acting thing down yet.

Can I skip it?

No, you cannot. These fun, lighthearted romps are mandatory.

What do I bring?

Not much, besides an immunity to small talk that is small on a microbial level.

How much do I drink?

The amount you'd consume on a first date, unless your first dates are often held at Pittsburgh sports bars.

What's the quickest way to ruin it?

Since your boss will indeed observe it through the Great Eye of Sauron if you're on your phone the whole time, mingling is highly encouraged. But not everybody in this ragtag unit is a master at the art of mingling (a Mingleangelo), and so there are inevitably lulls in each conversation. This is where the chance for disaster lives; where you're most likely to say the kind of things that inspire hilarious orientation videos. Avoid that outcome at all costs. Be more boring than you usually are. Talk about work, even though everybody thinks they hate that.

It's not exactly a good look to throw in the social towel and immediately start talking about work at a work party. Of course, some hero always glides in on a white horse to remind the first person who does it that, hey, we're off the clock, and we should leave business back at the office—a place we're currently inside right now. It's the kind of gently scolding meta-commentary no one can easily respond to. But at least it raises the chances that someone will say something totally inappropriate, just to fill the void, so that should be interesting.

House Party

What is it?

A house party, unlike most gatherings, actually *is* every party you see in the movies. Too many people. Too loud music. Too much drinking. It's a parody of fun. But sometimes also superfun.

Can I skip it?

Yes. Absolutely. No one will ever know. Every house party is like every other house party. Your memory basically files them all in one booze-soaked montage. If you're in the mood for a house party, show up. If you're not, don't. FOMOHP (Fear of Missing Out on a House Party) is negligible because you know exactly what you'd be getting.

What do I bring?

A reasonable guideline is "as much as you're going to drink, times two." But you can get away with showing up empty-handed if you don't mind drinking cheap beer and eating corn chips with no salsa or guacamole. Side note: Once you are older than twenty-five, Sam Adams is the minimum acceptable beer. No more Natural Ice or Milwaukee's Best. Those are for disciplinary beer bonging, and child shoplifters.

How much do I drink?

As much or as little as it takes.

What's the quickest way to ruin it?

Destroy someone's private property. Knock over a vase. Spill a drink on a white couch. Clog a toilet. Your options are limitless. Not only are these gaffes embarrassing, but you're obligated to fix them. Gross. Who needs that hassle?

Holiday Parties

What is it?

It's the most wonderful time of the year. Or that time of year that wasn't quite as wonderful for you as it was for the other kids, because of your parents' personal faith, but you're an adult now so anything goes, *Dad*.

Can I skip it?

Yes. Nobody likes to admit he or she is just fielding offers before making a shrewd executive decision, but everyone does that. The holiday season is *Shark Tank*. Your friends are the sharks, and you are the guy who invented a way to turn the gratuitous nudity on *Game of Thrones* into clean-burning energy. You've got options.

What do I bring?

Wine, side dish, childlike sense of wonder. More important, though, the right outfit. If you show up for Halloween in plain clothes or Cinco de Mayo without your formal sombrero, you'll be guilty of dress code insubordination. If it's an Ugly Christmas Sweater shindig, though, wear whatever feels most comfortable while looking for some new friends, because—whoops—your friends are terrible.

How much do I drink?

Until you sweat eggnog.

What's the quickest way to ruin it?

Unleash your food issues on the party like an airborne nerve agent. One thing all Easterpalooza and Memorial Day singles mixers have in common is bad food-related behaviors. Someone on a diet will narrate all the food offerings that he must refuse and how naughty everybody else is for eating them—as if the others are all in on doing a murder rather than enjoying slow-roasted carnitas sliders. The interest in what people are eating also extends to how much. Some self-appointed deputy of the Whole Foods salad bar nibble police will monitor the latke table with the urgency of Kevin Costner protecting Whitney Houston from stabby fans. Have you ever looked up from shoveling a chipload of queso in your face only to make eye contact with a food avenger? It may have been on accident, or it may come from a Marxist mandate for redistribution of dip, but either way one of you must now leave town forever.

Another holiday party food issue is what people can and can't eat. The newly converted will sometimes make their vegan debut during Thanksgiving, drawing attention to themselves about as much as a converted Jew wearing two yarmulkes at a Christmas party (side by side, a cranial infinity sign). Something about Thanksgiving especially lends itself to these kinds of us vs. them topics, guests taking sides while the host blithely tries to change the subject. The presence or absence of almond milk can be as contentious as a pro-life rally if certain people feel their food issues haven't been taken into account. As even more annoying allergies emerge—perhaps culminating in the Great Paprika Intolerance of 2016—and new trends infest the stalls of farmer's markets, these situations will probably just get worse.

Dinner Party

What is it?

A dinner party is real adult social interaction. It is composed of food and wine and conversation. It takes place at someone's house but is definitely not a "house party." Generally, a dinner party is big enough that you may not know some people but small enough that you'll have to talk to them anyway. Dinner guests will all be using their indoor voices.

Can I skip it?

You'll need a pretty solid excuse. It's likely you'll have RSVP'd by phone or e-mail, which, unlike a Facebook invitation, means people are actually counting on your attendance.

What do I bring?

A bottle of wine is a safe bet. It says: "I plan to enjoy fifteen to twenty-five dollars' worth of your company tonight." A pot-luck dinner is a different story. Here, you'll have an assignment and people are counting on you. You don't want to underdo it and bring mac and cheese from a box. At the same time, you don't want to go overboard and roast a pig if other people are showing up with a bag of Funyuns.

How much do I drink?

Read the room and keep pace with the other guests. Err on the side of, "I know all these people and ostensibly want to re-member this night."

What's the quickest way to ruin it?

Offend someone's significant other. No doubt about it. If you upset a friend, that can be repaired. If you piss off your friend's spouse, that's at least two people's nights you've ruined. Ask a buddy's husband, "Do you make a living at that?" when he de-scribes what he does for work. Tell a pal's girlfriend she's stupid and easily manipulated for still liking the movie *Slumdog Million-aire*. Call someone "sheeple."

Outdoor Parties

What is it?

Barbecues, picnics, roof parties, and beach bashes. Generally, these occur in the summer—all but guaranteeing people will see the part of your body you hate (the part with skin).

Can I skip it?

Yes. Hosts of outdoor parties don't care how many people show up. They're going to throw out most of the potato salad whether anyone else is around or not. It's gross.

What do I bring?

Sunblock, finger food, crappy beer that affords you an upgrade to somebody's better beer, crappy speakers for playing on-the-nose songs like Fresh Prince's "Summertime," and your own blanket that somebody will definitely plant half a butt cheek and a dollop of barbecue sauce on, which you will swear is totally fine even though it's not.

How much do I drink?

As much as you can handle. Everybody will be wearing sunglasses on sun-reddened faces, making those who drink like they mean it impossible to single out. A lot of outdoor parties take place in public, though, and they're not all in New Orleans, where the mayor is legally required to hold your left flank during

a keg stand. It takes only one shotgunned beer to get the entire
picnic ticketed, and then you become a party pariah.

What's the quickest way to ruin it?

Bring an alpha intensity to the proceedings. Since you're
outside and the weather is gorgeous, you're expected to participate in activities, rather than just sit there formally accepting
the sun's toxins. The person who doesn't play Frisbee comes
across like nonjoining dead weight, whereas the way-too-into-it
guy seems to be compensating for a fatherly game of catch that
never happened.

Friend's Birthday

What is it?

For an adult, a birthday is less an ice cream cake and party
hat affair and more an excuse to bring friends together for a
night of shared merriment, often at some bar. But if anyone got
their hands on an ice cream cake, nobody would hate that. Occasionally, the night will involve both dinner and drinks at a second location. In that case, you can pick one or the other to
attend. Some people extend their friends' goodwill into a "birthday week" celebration, but those people are monsters. We shall
speak no more of them.

Can I skip it?

It's a complicated algorithm, the birthday party. The closer the friend, the harder the party is to miss. The bigger the party, the easier it is to bail. The more intimate the invitation, the tougher it is to avoid (a phone call being the most compelling invitation, public Facebook status being the least.) Even Einstein would've had trouble with this issue if he'd been allowed by the government to make any friends.

What do I bring?

Your presence is usually enough of a present, but be prepared to split the cost of the guest of honor's dinner or booze. In fact, be ready to split the bill evenly if it's a dinner. It's a sneaky way for some people to subsidize their seafood and wine on everyone else's dime. Stay alert!

How much do I drink?

No one's paying attention and everyone's splitting the check, so just keep up with the friend closest to hitting rock bottom so you can be sure you're getting your money's worth.

What's the quickest way to ruin it?

Upset the birthday guest. Everything else is negotiable. As long as the celebrant is happy, the party will be a success. Making a disparaging comment about the guest of honor's age seems fun, but, really, no one loves being reminded of her own mortality on a night she is supposedly celebrating. Or, for a shot of awkwardness straight to the jugular, wait until the birthday gal is a little buzzed and then mention how you ran into her most recent ex and he was looking superhappy and had a hot new romantic interest.

Family Gatherings

What is it?

A family is a circle of people who love, talk about, and judge each other constantly. Let's spend some time with those fuckers!

Can I skip it?

Only if you're actively trying to break your poor mother's heart, you jerk.

What do I bring?

The same items warmly welcomed at some parties might be deemed passive-aggressive insults at others. Your aunt may interpret your bringing a quiche to her anniversary party as a gesture condemning not only her cooking abilities but every decision she's ever made, including marrying your uncle.

How much do I drink?

Enough to convince your teenage cousin that you can hang, even though he or she will never be able to relay the message back to the classmates who christened you the Virginator when you were that age.

What's the quickest way to ruin it?

Hijack someone's big moment by making it about you. Telling guests big news during your sister's bat mitzvah sends the message that your sister does not matter and that you refuse to recognize her agency as an adult Jewish woman. Revealing too much about yourself is just as problematic as revealing family secrets. Tell one person which of your cousins in attendance is in the middle of a clandestine divorce and watch the tension in the air escalate. Now the party has become a *Real Housewives* episode or a cat-and-mouse espionage thriller during which you may be exposed as a mole.

Another way to turn a family function into a fiasco is to try too hard to get people to do stuff. Like the person who was unable to get a conga line started at a work party, somebody at a family event usually will try to make everybody converge on the dance floor on Mom's living room carpet. Just remember that "Everybody Dance Now" should be a suggestion from C+C Music Factory, not a command. If you can't make your family do a thing, that doesn't mean try harder until you wear down their resistance. These people have built up a lifetime of resistance to you, like someone carefully cultivating an immunity to poison.

Bachelor/Bachelorette Party

What is it?

One last hurrah before a friend gets married.

Can I skip it?

You can, but your friends will make you feel like a hot summer Dumpster until there's someone else to pick on. Women do it with guilt ("It would mean *so much* if you could be there"), and men do it by chanting "puuuuusssssyyyyy" until you hit them or they lose custody of their kids.

What do I bring?

A willingness to do the worst, tackiest things without complaint. A bachelor or bachelorette party may compel you to do any of the following: visit a strip club, drink from straws shaped like penises, drink the kind of booze you buy when you're underage, wear a crown shaped like a collection of braided penises, play a sport neither you nor your friends have played in years, or go on a scavenger hunt for the penises of college students.

How much do I drink?

A lot. Being a sober person at one of these parties is like being drunk at work: Sure you *can* do it, but people are going to notice, and even if they say nothing, they'll treat you like you're a spy for the other wedding party, and exclude you from penis cake or boob pierogies or any other foods shaped like body parts.

What's the quickest way to ruin it?

Puncture the illusion that you're having the best night of your life. Of course, you don't *want* to be cramming money down the underwear of a stranger whose name is an adjective. No one *likes* having to scream "Woooo!" and smoosh seven people into a selfie. But to acknowledge that what you're doing is the opposite of how you choose to spend your time literally every other day of the year is to negate the specialness of the evening and deny your friend the freest possible last night of freedom.

Wedding

What is it?

Two of your friends are joining together in beautiful, holy matrimony. Or maybe it's one friend and a person you met a couple of times. Perhaps it's a childhood friend you haven't seen in years and a new spouse you've never even heard of. Maybe someone your significant other went to college with got someone pregnant after dating for three weeks, and now you have to buy them a blender. Regardless of the participants, two people are committing to spend the rest of their lives together, a promise that proves to be a lie 50 percent of the time.

Can I skip it?

Oof. Probably not. If someone is inviting you to a wedding, then that person considers you a close friend and would prefer that you be there. Except, of course, in the case where someone is trying to "pizza-slice" you—that is, invite you out of obligation, the way you offer someone the last pizza slice, hoping they'll decline. Also, a destination wedding is easier to say no to. If you don't know, a destination wedding is when a couple loves each other so much that they decide their friends need to celebrate by spending half their net worth on a weekend trip to Turks and Caicos.

What do I bring?

Technically, etiquette says you have a year to deliver on a wedding gift, but don't be an asshole. Just bring a gift to the reception. Try to find something on the registry that is equivalent to the cost of the dinner you'll be eating there, but don't literally offer them your untouched wedding dinner and yell, "Congratulations!"

How much do I drink?

How much *can* you drink? A quick word of caution, though. An open bar, much like a buffet, seems like an invitation to try to recoup your travel expenses one glass of wine at a time. *Do not* take the bait. It will bring you nothing but heartache, despair, and Facebook pics of you doing MC Hammer's signature dance, the Typewriter.

What's the quickest way to ruin it?

Most weddings are big enough that even fairly inappropriate gestures can get swept under the rug. You'll be fine unless you do something so outrageous that it attracts the attention of the entire gathering. Egregious behaviors include falling through the cake, trying to tongue-kiss the bride or groom, sobbing and blowing your nose on the bouquet, and giving a rambling toast that quotes Lil Jon. Remember, unless you've become the focus of the whole party, you're in the clear. So behave yourself!

Being the Host with the Most (Obligations)

Sometimes, instead of attending a party, you are in a position of planning one of your own. Perhaps it's your birthday, or the birthday of a loved one. Maybe it's even your own wedding. (Congratulations and good luck! Forget the thing we said about 50 percent of marriages failing!) In addition to the fulfillment that comes with successfully throwing a gathering for friends and loved ones, it also provides so many novel ways to turn the whole thing into a circus of nightmares for every attendee.

As a host, you're still constrained by the tight dress pants of politeness, the same as any guest. But you're also responsible for the caliber of fun had by everyone. A few things to consider:

Timing

You're going to want to plan your event for a time when people are free, but not *too* free. Fewer people will show up at your birthday brunch if you have it on a weeknight. However, if you plan a going-away party on the Fourth of July weekend, everyone else will have beaten you to the idea of getting out of town. You don't want to compete with any other parties either, which could lead to your Halloween costume bash falling in mid-October to avoid conflict, *or* meeting the conflict head-on by parading all your guests through the streets, "Beat It"–style, for a gang war against Karen's party.

Location

For a house party, obviously, you can just fall back on your home, but any other soiree entails picking a place. There are so many considerations: What restaurants have nut-free menus? Which bar can accommodate the number of people you're planning to bring? If you're scheduling an outdoor event, do you know the right ancient prayer or reverse–rain dance to ensure nice weather until your BBQ is over? Is there public transportation? Is there parking? Bike racks? Skateboard docks? Rollerblade cubbies? Hoverboard chargers? Is the venue centrally located, or at least located closest to the person who complains the most about travel?

Refreshments

Again, it's a tightrope. You don't want to underprepare and end up with a party full of hungry, sober, cranky guests. But you don't want to get a banquet ready only to find out your friends already ate (who eats before seven P.M.????) and are just planning to nibble on a carrot stick so you don't feel bad. (You didn't go to any trouble, did you? Of course you did!) Now you're stuck with six bags of corn chips, which is five and a half more bags than any one person would need in a lifetime. Same with alcohol. You don't want to run out of beverages, causing your friends to pour out of your home like air escaping a slashed tire—a tire that likely belongs to the host of a suddenly dry party. You also don't want to buy a keg and then feel the pressure to finish it yourself after everyone decides they're "taking it easy after New Year's." Drinking from a keg when you're alone may not specifically be a sign of alcoholism, but it's certainly a signifier that things could be better.

Guests

The second-most important question for planning any party is who to invite. The most important is who *not* to invite. Addition by subtraction is a common theme in professional sports; it's the idea that by removing a problematic presence from the locker room, you're actually enhancing the team. Parties are the same. You need to prune your guest list like a hedge or else it will overgrow into the neighbors' yard, where they will cut it with a chainsaw even though they could have just *told you* it was bothering them. Clearly, you want to keep invitations out of the hands of the unfun: creeps, drunks, anybody who is never without a Settlers of Catan travel–size board game. You're also going to want to make sure the cast of characters is compatible (no recent exes, no people who used to work together until one got fired for embezzling).

All in all, you may just be better off living a life completely unworthy of celebration.

Familiar Faces and How Not to Remeet Them

It's always great to meet new people! Okay, often great! Well, sometimes great!

What's less exciting is meeting someone you've already met for the second or, yikes, third time, but don't quite remember. Nothing overtly says, "I'm more memorable to you than you are to me!" like forgetting someone's name (or his or her significant other's name, as we mentioned earlier). Well, except for these ill-advised responses:

1. "We've met."

There is no colder greeting than a flat, icy, "We've met." What that really means is, "I can't believe you don't remember that we've met." And even if that's true, nobody wins when you start a conversation there. It becomes a pissing contest. And those always end with two sets of wet feet.

2. "We definitely haven't met."

Oh, haven't you? That is a *strong* wager to come out with, considering there's no way you remember every face that's ever said ten words to you. "We definitely haven't met," really means, "If we have met, you were so unimpressive, I didn't even remember you. And I remember several Pitbull lyrics that I don't even like." (Everyone does.)

3. "Oh my gosh, what does your driver's license look like?"

That trick seemed genius in college, but adults will roll their eyes at you like you started playing "got your nose."

4. "How do you spell your name again?"
Great trick if you're chatting with a Marc/Mark or a Katie/
Catie/Katy.

Less applicable if you're running into a Bob or a Lisa or—
and this apparently happens more often than you might
expect—third-tier porn star the Gooch.

5. "Oh! You used to date [fill in the blank]!"
No! No! No! No! Abort! Abort! Imagine if someone said
that to you. Mortifying, right? "You used to date Tom!" Yeah,
and now you're there with your current significant other
who *hates* Tom or, even worse, *has never even heard about*
Tom—until now. Do *not* reintroduce yourself this way unless
you want the whole social structure of the evening to
tumble to the floor like a figure skater who sprained her
ankle trying to skate away from you too fast.

Exit Wounds: The Worst Ways to Leave a Party

Even if you've managed to make it through the party without
making a spectacle of yourself, there's still plenty of time to
snatch defeat from the jaws of victory. How you make your exit
matters, too. These are the ways to do so that will help ensure
you don't get invited back:

> **Irish Good-bye:** Vanish into the night, possibly stranding
> the people you came with and sparking rumors of kid-
> napping and randomly placed trapdoors.
> **Jewish Good-bye:** Repeatedly tell the host that if it were
> anyone else's party, you'd have definitely left already
> because you need to get up early, but hey, what's one

sleepless night—until she finally feels guilty enough to demand that you leave.

The Barnacle: Refuse to take hints until eventually the host explains outright that it is the end of the night and you're about as welcome as an enormous bedbug.

The Grizzly: Drunkenly pass out and hibernate like a bear and then wake up the next afternoon and devour raw salmon from a nearby brook.

The Benedict Arnold: Leave early to go to another party that you've clearly decided is the better party.

The Grand Finale: Tell at least one person how you *really* feel and storm out dramatically while wearing an opera cape.

The Repo Man: Stake a claim on the leftover alcohol or food you brought and bring it home—possibly in a grocery bag, for the sake of thematic symmetry.

The False Alarm: Say good-bye a number of times and then change your mind, confronting everyone you've already said good-bye to with the horrific possibility of having to do it again.

LOVE AND/OR SEX

CHAPTER 5

Sometimes You Play the Field and Sometimes the Field Plays You

It would be nice if you could bypass dating entirely. You'd meet someone at a sporting goods store, discover you hate the same stuff, and jump right into couplehood, possibly right there in the camping accessories aisle. But it's never going to happen that way. While the process of getting to know people, and possibly sleeping with them, has completely changed in recent years, you still have to go through the weeks-long Choose Your Own Adventure–style romantic decathlon of finding a suitable mate—only now it's mostly done remotely.

Before the iPhone, Apple Watch, and inevitable upcoming iBrain Chip Implant, we had to actually go on dates if we wanted to ruin them. There were, of course, some inadvisable, untakebackable answering machine messages. (You know, back when listening to a voice mail wasn't less enticing than hearing an a cappella Avicii concert.) Now, there are digital booby traps constantly putting us in romantic peril. We carry tiny machines whose powers are indistinguishable from the dark arts. And much like young wizard-school pupils, we must maintain constant vigilance against our most powerful enemies: ourselves (not to mention whiskey).

The Internet has an indelible dossier of every dumb thing we've done since the early 2000s, all just a Google away—or maybe a Bing, if you're a weirdo. (And if your secrets aren't cataloged for the whole world to see—who even are you, some kind of assassin?) Though our dating pools are larger than ever, we must now worry more about the pH level of the water, because it's easier to pee in there.

Stranger Danger: The Horror of Meeting New People

As we've just implied, the meet-cute as you know it is dead. Unless you live in an early nineties romantic comedy, you aren't going to bump into the love of your life while you're both carrying overstuffed sacks of baguettes, spilling your groceries all over the floor, and then engaging in spontaneous baguette fencing. We meet people online, or we start dating friends of friends. Why? Because strangers are often smelly and rude and occasionally murderous. Pursuing a meet-cute, the adorable, quirky story that connects you and your future beloved for the first time, is not just tacky, it could also be tragic.

Here are a few strategies that may help you find a mate if you're in a movie, but not in real life:

- Maybe the rude bank teller is just trying to get your attention. Withdraw one dollar every day until she gets the courage to ask you out.

- If someone tries to shutter your spunky, independent business, win him over by making a mixtape.
- That crying baby who ruins your whole cross-country flight? Wait until she is a legal adult and then take her out for coffee to reminisce.
- Track down the guy who stole your credit card information from a fake PayPal site and ask him out.
- If a shark bites you while you're surfing, bake it cookies.
- Bang your landlord.
- When a Terminator arrives from the future to murder your son, uncork a bottle of wine and laugh about how different you are.

The point is, you can't just expect you'll fall in love with someone because he or she is your enemy—like opposing lawyers played by George Clooney and Sandra Bullock, who hate each other at first until they realize their genitals were made for each other in some weird laboratory. We can't all be that lucky.

In olden times, such as 2003, if you wanted to learn about someone you'd just met, you had to trust the euphemistic descriptions of mutual friends. You'd hear all about the "super nice" person who actually has no social skills, or someone who's "a *lot* of fun" and turns out to be an inhibition-free maniac prone to midparty crying jags. Thank goodness for Facebook. It's CliffsNotes for people. You can learn a lot about the relative dateworthiness of strangers just from their pages—their politics, their taste in music, and their particular idea of what details are okay to disclose publicly. Moreover, you can learn what they look like in a curated series of photos. Click carefully, though, lest you accidentally "like" a bathing suit pic from the photo album "Summertime and the Living's Easy 2008" and have to cut off all communication with this person forever.

Some may cast aspersions on this type of reconnaissance. They call it "creeping" or "Facebook stalking"—both misnomers that take something away from actual perverts with binoculars who are willing to put in the legwork. So-called Facebook stalking is something everybody does. It just happens to have a name that's also a form of assault. What not everybody does, though, is get caught peeping red-handed, like George McFly spying on his teenage future bride, Lorraine, in *Back to the Future*—a movie that weirdly asks us to continue rooting for George after that happens. (Choose whoever you want, Lorraine! Choose Biff! He doesn't even know what binoculars are!) Any proof of trawling through someone's photographic deep cuts on Facebook shows you're way more interested than you should be.

Even if someone is off Facebook (a trendy place to be these days), a cursory Internet search should yield the pertinent details: notable places of employment, newsworthy run-ins with the law, or published personal essays about men's rights activism. You can get a feel for what we'd call someone's "personal brand" if that phrase didn't make us want to burn a PR firm to the ground.

Save the Date (So You Can Ruin It Later)

There used to be only two ways to ask someone out: throwing pebbles against a bedroom window in the night or calling a landline. Those were the days! Without caller ID, you could ring someone up infinite times, and if he or she didn't answer, there was no way to know you'd called. As long as the object of your affection didn't dig through the trash for a phone bill, there was no record of your neurotic lunacy. (And if she or he was in fact doing that, you two were made for each other!) The pebble method was riskier, though. One shattered window is at least as bad as a thousand embarrassing answering machine messages.

Now we have constant access to each other, and every form of communication leaves a trail. Missed calls leave a log line. Unanswered text messages slowly build up into novellas of desperation. E-mails are time-stamped. Why were you even *awake* at 4:30 A.M., never mind checking up on someone you've never met? And what's with all the "praise hands" emoji? Are you in cyborg church?

The movie *Swingers* ignited public debate about how long one should wait to call a potential romantic partner. But that movie was set in a quaint era called 1996, several inches ago along Vince Vaughn's hairline. Even the characters in that film who played it cool by waiting six days to call would now seem like needy creeps. How long does one wait to call now? Trick question. You *never* call!

At this point in history, a telephone conversation is as invasive as a full cavity search. Humans have grown unaccustomed to casual chats over the phone. We use delivery.com to order our meals. We exchange e-mails with our best friends. We Skype in sick to work. We have so many avenues for getting in touch these days, it's impossible to be sure you're not accidentally pinging NFL player D'Brickashaw Ferguson *right now*. If you're under forty years old, a telephone call means one of two things: a customer service nightmare or your mom. Do you want to be seen as either of those things by someone you hope to see naked?

Chemistry Test: Where Not to Go on a First Date

Spontaneity is a virtue, but a first date is like auditioning for *Survivor*. You don't tell your parents you're doing it, and you need a backup plan. While you shouldn't rehearse your date using tiny dolls and a restaurant diorama, there's no excuse for not preparing at all. Maybe you could get away with that in the 1950s, when there was only one restaurant per town and every table was reserved in case Frank Sinatra showed up, but not in these crazy times. Merely having a plan isn't enough, though, because the only thing worse than a freestyle date is having a plan that sucks.

Your first date is basically a pre-date to determine whether being around each other in the flesh makes either of you want to barf everywhere. Ergo, anything above the level of a simple sampling of food or alcohol is too grandiose. Mismatched date expectations stand out as much as a tuxedo jacket paired with sweatpants, and neither is a good look. Having too much riding on a first date sends the message that if this doesn't work out, it's all over for you and you're just barely hanging on by a thread. Being underprepared is also poor form, though. Wow, sometimes it's amazing we've managed to keep repopulating the earth for so long.

Here are some examples of where not to go on a first date:

One of Your Apartments

If you can get someone to come to your home, you have already overcome the number one obstacle to romance: the fear that you are a deranged lunatic. However, nothing sets off the deafening alarm bells of fight or flight faster than a premature attempt to bring someone into an unfamiliar residence, alone.

Drinks and More Drinks and More Drinks

Drinks make an ideal date because they give you something to do with your hands and inhibitions. *But* too many drinks can ruin the whole thing because it could lead to embarrassing honesty you meant to hide. Or, God forbid, the other person will reveal something about himself that makes you not want to sleep with him. Don't get too liquored up or you'll end up sharing/ hearing third-date-level secrets before you've even been naked together. Seeing each other's nude bodies is *mutually* embarrassing. It keeps you on a level playing field.

Dinner at an Unacceptable Place

Dinner is like drinks because you can get drunk at it, but it's different than drinks because it costs more and you'll probably get schmutz on your face. There are two things to know about dinner, though: Don't sit next to each other in a booth because it looks like you're a couple who took their son's ghost out to dinner (unbeknownst to them), and don't pick out a lousy restaurant just because it's in your price range or close proximity.

You're going on a first date, not meeting with an ex to give back a box of T-shirts.

Some Random Movie

Movies are not great for conventional first dates. Aside from the potential for watching explicit sex scenes next to a stranger, you can't talk to your date at all. So when you're done, you need an additional "first date." You might as well have taken a nap near the other person for all you've learned about her. A movie is a great way to *feel like* you're on a date without ever having to interact or reveal anything about yourself or connect with a human person on any level. Also, most movies, like most people, are garbage.

A Walk

Yeah, sure. Walking sounds fun. It's a nice day. You'll just wander the city until you see something that seems worth eating or looking at. *What could possibly go wrong* except for an entire day of ceaseless, chemistryless boredom and soreness and hunger? Nothing, nothing more than that.

You Lost Me at "Hello": First-Date Red Flags

So much has to go right in order for a first date to work out that you have better odds of trying to land a plane with only rudimentary knowledge of aeronautics. Think about it: Just one really powerful sneeze could potentially crash your date-plane into an awkward mountain. So it's better to focus on the things you can control, you poor, congested dork.

By now, you've researched your date's Internet presence like you were cramming for midterms. And your date has researched yours. Now comes the hard part: denying this ever happened. Treat your online recon like an Ivy League education. Let it inform your decisions, but for the love of God, don't talk about it. On a first date, saying "I saw that on Facebook" seems less likely to have come from a charming, interested acquaintance than from a wolf dressed up as your grandma.

This next one is just for the men. Ladies, please exit the book. Is it just us fellas now? Good. You know that stuff guys in movies always do during dates? Chivalry and all that classy shit? Women in real life hate it so much. Everything from making a big show out of opening the big, scary restaurant door to finding out what dates want and ordering for them—it's all patronizing. It's been patronizing all along, but earlier generations of women were too busy feeling psyched about simply not being sold to a husband like cattle that they failed to notice. While this stuff certainly impresses some women, others just take it as proof that you read and memorized a getting-laid playbook and you're running drills right now. Don't deprive your date of the experience of interacting with a server. Maybe he'll understand her in ways you were never meant to, and it will be a romance for the ages. Not letting your date talk to the waiter looks as if you're trying to stand in the way of destiny.

Coming on too strong instead of treating a date like a blossoming friendship is something else that trips people up. Remember making friends? It's what we did when we were frightened children who hadn't met other people yet. Try more of that. While bragging about how you are crushing it in every aspect of life is not an attractive quality, neither is self-deprecation that turns your date into its own Friars roast. An aggressive personality is just as bad as a neurotic one, because loving and hating yourself too much are two sides of the same worthless, self-obsessed coin. Keep the change!

Okay, enough of the man talk. Ladies, please return to the book. Anyway, a date isn't a job interview for sex, despite all the glaring similarities between the two processes. (See "Exit Interview for an Online Date" in the next chapter.) It's less about impressing the other person with qualifications and secret clerical superpowers than it is about determining compatibility. It's a night out. Have some good old-fashioned fun with your new friend.

"We Should Totally Do This Again Sometime"

When a first date seems to be going well, your natural instinct is to follow it up as soon as possible. But pulling out your Gcalendar before the date is officially over makes you seem as eager as a recent parolee. No matter how naturally the conversation drifts toward some upcoming movie/art exhibit/drum circle, anything more than vaguely gesturing toward it as a thing you might do together suggests that you consider this first date a down payment. This is a video game to you, and making it past the first level means you've won ten sex favors and a plump satchel of gold doubloons. You're practically pointing at your date's ass and high-fiving passersby.

On the other hand, waiting too long to text afterward is just as off-putting. A secret agent might be able to get away with going off the grid after a nice date and hollering a couple of weeks later. If James Bond has taught us anything, it's that spies are constantly getting it on with sexy henchpeople and other spies, rather than the public at large, so being in no hurry to reconnect makes sense. Mere civilians, though, should get in touch within a couple of days or never again.

If the first date is just for trying to establish whether there is even a chance you have chemistry, the second is when you experiment with the Erlenmeyer flask of sexual attraction. As unjust as it sounds to the supercautious, you can blow it on the second date by waiting so long for the right moment to make a move that now all the moments are gone and you're on your deathbed, wondering how all these grandkids got here after a lifetime of near virginity.

So be careful, but not too careful. Flubbing the follow-up makes it so the initial date might as well have never happened, turning you into the unreliable narrator in a novel about a person who is terrible at dating.

Or, maybe you don't want anything serious. In that case:

One Night Only: How to Stop a Casual Hookup from Blossoming into Something More

- Put a wedding ring on immediately after sex.
- Give a fake name . . . to the other person. "Nice to meet you, Dave." "I'm Salvatore." "Not tonight."
- Leave through the window.
- Enter through the window.

- Be the kind of person who has a sword over your bed.
- Do the *Law & Order* or *SportsCenter* chime when you orgasm.
- Take the sheets off the bed before lovemaking and say, "You understand."
- Wink. A lot.
- Grab the other guy's erection like you're throwing a switch and scream: "IT'S ALIVE!"
- Leave behind an item of clothing, a toothbrush, and a live animal.

CHAPTER 6

Love in the Time of OkCupid

A fun thing to do is study the face of a person explaining that he met his girlfriend online. The vocal strain and eyebrow gymnastics betray a kind of embarrassment and defeat common among animals mating in captivity. Heed not the actual words, for these are surely lies. Instead, soak in the telekinetic SOSs ordering you to switch subjects.

It's a cruel joke most people never see coming when they anoint a laptop to be their sexual concierge: that it will actually succeed, only to then attract constant questions about how that happened. Even when it seems you've *won* at online dating, the close-tab button on your success remains but a left-click away.

The stigma around online dating initially stemmed from its newness. Dating sites were mysteries and also evidence of sweeping social change—a combo that proved irresistible to skeptics. "No thanks, computer bordello!" your average Match. com holdout might've said. "There is literally nothing I don't love about making myself available in sweaty bars at closing time." By now, though, this stigma has evolved into a totally different stigma. People no longer dislike online dating out of ignorance but from firsthand experience and post-traumatic stress disorder. We're all in the same secret club together, greeting each other with the same handshake (it's when you press your Tinder-swiping fingers together like E.T. and Elliott).

Whether you admit it or not, though, sometimes your so-called horror story about online dating is just that you failed at it. Some prospects seem too good to be true but actually *are* that good—and then, in the ultimate M. Night Shyamalan twist, it turns out *you* are the one who is not good enough. People always advise nervous daters, "Just be yourself." However, the more your self is weighed against a meticulously fussed-over salad buffet version online, the greater the chance your house of cards will fall down and burst into flames. Let's take a look at some of the many reasons why you might become someone else's reason to hate online dating.

Rank and (Pro)file: Getting Started

A dating profile is your chance to emphasize the best qualities of the person you pretend to be, in order to entice people who have no idea what they really want. Lately, though, geolocational dating apps like Tinder have rendered profiles largely irrelevant. Why scour a stack of self-portraits painted with half-truths when you can simply ping everyone in a three-mile radius? Hot singles in your area are looking to copulate, and you can join them right now! But for those who still rely on dating sites that don't use global positioning, a personality-filled profile can be the difference maker.

Online dating is a smorgasbord of snap judgments and no second chances. The quicker you eliminate individuals as potential love connections, the quicker three nearly identical people emerge to take their place like sexy whack-a-mole. As the automatic dismissals pile up, revealing that you do in fact have a "type," you begin to refine whom you really are interested in. Some of these folks will be fast-tracked into the messaging stage because of sheer hotness, but for everyone else, a profile that doesn't suck is how you level up.

Of course, men and women tend to blow it on their dating profiles in different ways. Both might boast about their juice-cleansed lifestyle until you feel like smacking the vitamin-rich smirk off their faces, and either one might rattle off a smug, endless list of things interested parties shouldn't do. Rather than reveal our own list of deal breakers, though, we've assembled composite profiles for any gender. These hypothetical folks say what nobody of the opposite sex (or hey, the same sex) wants to hear, bringing you the worst of both worlds.

My details:

User name: DatWangTho

Last time online: Right now

Orientation: Not Adam and Steve. Those guys both have
    penises.

Ethnicity: We're all the same when the lights go out.

Height: 5'9"

Body type: Sick

Diet: Def not vegan. Do I look like I make gentle love to tree
   bark using ballerina slippers?

Smokes? Not cigarettes ;)

Drinks? Um, you might say that I . . . exhibit some early
   symptoms of alcoholism, heh.

Drugs? I can't remember, lol

Religion: Is MMA a religion?

Astrological sign: Dunno

Education: Community College of Hard Knocks, in Dirty Jerz

Job: A wolf cub of Wall Street

Income: I'm rich, beyotch!

Relationship status: Horny AF

My self-summary:

I'm a misunderstood nice guy who's looking for a down-to-
   earth girl—and by down-to-earth, I mean down to
   clown. Every woman I've dated has historically been a
   backstabbing gold-digging prostitute, but maybe you
   are different, or at least hot.

What I'm doing with my life:

Living it to the fullest and pushing it to the limit. #Blessed

I'm really good at:

U'll see. ;)

The first thing people usually notice about me:

My tattoo of John Wayne beating up the moon.

Favorite books, movies, shows, music, food:

Everything except country and opera. That goes for all the above, especially food.

The six things I could never do without:

Sex ;) Oxygen. lol. Do you get it? Because you literally could not live without a functional respiratory system. #Winning. My phone. My father, and the prospect of fighting him. #Blessed

I spend a lot of time thinking about:

Where we all came from. What it all means. What kind of cruel god would bestow unto a person so much love, and keep the proper love-receptacle so well hidden?

The most private thing I'm willing to admit:

I'd very much like you to admit my private thing into yours. Lol.

I'm looking for:

A down-to-earth chick who likes to party but isn't a party girl and likes sex but isn't a slut and believes in binary systems for defining people but isn't defined by them.

On a typical Friday night I am:

Bonin' like the earth's population depends on it. My go-to fantasy for this scenario is that the *Planet of the Apes* movies are real, and if we don't get it on, mankind will be torn asunder by filthy monkeys. So yeah, you could say I sex pretty hard.

You should message me if:

You're a real chick who doesn't play games. Specifically, not rugby or Scrabble. Lol.

My details:

User name: KellyOnMyWaywardSon
Last time online: Right now
Orientation: Uhhh, at least buy me dinner first.
Ethnicity: Sauvignon Blanc
Height: 5'4"
Body type: Curvy but like a thin curvy
Diet: Death before carbs
Smokes? Nopes
Drinks? Ya thinks?
Drugs? Ughs
Religion: Spiritual
Astrological sign: Libra with Scorpio tendencies
Education: Every day I learn something from this big wonderful world of wonders.
Job: Marketing assistant
Income: —
Relationship status: Just one singular sensation

My self-summary:

I love life and I love to laugh. My friend Madison made me do this; the idea of online dating repulses me at a core level. Each of you is probably a gross and deeply flawed homunculus who will try to keep me in his creepy sex dungeon. But loving life as I do, why should I keep myself closed off from new experiences, especially ones that might help me get married before my little sister does? Oh and yes I'm aware that the user name I picked is almost explicitly Oedipal, and if I'd realized I couldn't change it, I'd have picked something else.

What I'm doing with my life:

Trying to experience everything the big city has to offer— when I'm not traveling, that is! I aspire to make a difference in the world, one hashtag at a time.

I'm really good at:

Yoga. Hugs. Brunch. Keeping up with the Kardashians. Really working on *me* right now.

The first thing people usually notice about me:

My smile. A quiet confidence. My . . . assets. Lol. The sun glinting off of my hair as I skip stones across a Central Park stream at sunset and picture a world without poverty.

Favorite books, movies, shows, music, food:

Fifty Shades of Nicholas Sparks; movies with monkeys, Muppets, and/or Meryl; RuPaul's Housewife Races; OneRepublican Direction; brunch

The six things I could never do without:

My girls. My French bulldog, Taco. My phone. Yoga.
Brunch-travel. Everything this city has to offer.

I spend a lot of time thinking about:

How I'm going to fill this thing out. Lol.

The most private thing I'm willing to admit:

I often cry when I sense that somewhere a penguin might
be in danger.

I'm looking for:

"A body like Arnold with a Denzel face." —Salt-N/or-Pepa

On a typical Friday night I am:

Either out and about, experiencing life as it was meant to
be lived, or staying in and using a blow-dryer to sail little
plastic boats across the water in a bathtub regatta.

You should message me if:

You like what you've read so far, you're funny, you're not
judgmental, and not short.

Pics or It Isn't Happening: Your Profile Picture

Choosing pictures for your online dating profile is like curating a museum of yourself or, as we call it, a "youseum." The trick is including a shrewd balance of portraiture, still life, and tasteful nudes. Okay, maybe not the nudes. The goal in arranging your youseum is to make people want to get the hell out of there and meet you, not stick around and gawk.

Australia's Aborigines believe that getting your picture taken steals a piece of your soul. Fortunately, everyone else believes that taking selfies is like mainlining a lagoon's worth of James Brown–level bonus soul. Selfies are photography's guitar solos, expressions of individuality that in no way signify people don't want to have their picture taken with you. While having too many on your profile might be frowned upon, it still beats posting a bunch of group shots that force people to play Where's Waldo? with no idea what Waldo even looks like.

It also hurts to include a surplus of photos featuring the competition—members of the desired sex who are so attractive that they've likely never considered online dating. Guys are notorious for seeding in photos of themselves with random hot women, usually while making a sideways peace sign so potential dates know they're into hand gestures *and* the diplomacy of President Nixon. Women are more likely to include photos of exes whose faces are scratched out in a way that suggests bayou voodoo. Whoever the other people are in profile photos, they're just window dressing, so those faces might as well be wineglasses or Bengal tigers or anything else that isn't an unexplained baby.

Way too many online daters try hiding what they consider

flaws either through body tilting, high angles, or more filters and lens flares than a J. J. Abrams space opera. Using special effects in photos may raise doubts about your aesthetic authenticity, but it's not as embarrassing as making the same expression in every picture like a cyborg stuck on "sultry." Even if you do attract someone's attention with your misguided photos, though, the odds are you'll lose it while exchanging messages.

Making a Mess(age)

Scrolling through profiles is like trying to decide what to watch on Netflix. Everything looks okay and there's so much available that it all blends together into one low-budget heist movie starring Nicolas Cage. As you continue to click, though, your baseline for contacting someone lowers. You learn the exact threshold of interesting or hot you're willing to explore. Pretty soon you send messages with the open-minded optimism of Nic Cage's agent flagging potential starring roles. So begins the pursuit.

Whether people admit it or not, everybody loves the thrill of the chase. With online dating, however, the chase slows to a crawl, and everyone conducts multiple pursuits at the same time. It's total chaos. Instead of focusing their thirst into a tactical drone strike or two, a lot of guys roll in like a fleet of General Pattons and carpet bomb the perimeter. Unfortunately for them, they also make it crazy obvious that they're doing exactly that.

The first message is critical. It kicks off your formal campaign for the office of sexual congress. Coming up with a thoughtful, clever opener tailored to each person is hard work, but it works better than sending the same form letter to whoever meets the minimum criteria. An impersonal overture usually comes across that way, and is as easy to spot as a cold sore.

When contacting a guy, you can get away with a first message that's basically some version of, "I notice that you, too, are a living person. Care to comment?" When writing to a woman, however, it's better to convey at least some glimmer of personality beyond the word "'Sup." The only sin worse than disregarding what's in a profile, or being boring, is pointing out that today is, in fact, hump day, or making any number of other clunky premature bone-down offers. You can just assume these will be screen-shot and disseminated among a coterie of friends who relish any opportunity to make fun of you.

Once you finally send out a message, simply check for a response every five seconds until your phone is worn down to what's known as a Cupertino nubbin. All there is to do now is lean back and relax—so you can say you *tried* to do that before obsessively rereading the sent message until you figure out not only where you went wrong with it but also with life itself.

Some people advise against sending more messages when you haven't heard back on the first, but those people have no sense of adventure. Go ahead. Knock yourself out. Are you one of those people who like to dig themselves into a deep hole just to see if they can climb out? We've heard of those. Keep digging! Faster!

From E-Meet to See Meat

The sooner you actually get together, the easier it is to trick your brain into forgetting you ordered each other from an Internet menu of people. If you've exchanged messages a couple of times, you're both probably up for seeing each other in the harsh light of day/reality. Once an offer is extended, though, there's no guarantee you'll actually go through with it. Some online romances curdle in the process of getting to that first date, like if Pinocchio died midway through his transformation, a half-wooden corpse-puppet.

The thing about online dating is that even when it feels like it's going well, the other shoe could drop at any time. Something might suddenly change and make clear why this person used the Internet to get a date instead of letting nature take its course. It can even happen before you've ever met.

After making a date with someone you met online, you should simply shut up and relax. Checking in too much seems pesky and desperate, like you can't believe your luck and now you're pinching yourself to make sure this is not just a wonderful dream. But each pre-date text is more like pinching the other person, and nobody likes being pinched. Who even pinches anymore? Why did we ever do that? Anyway, the point is you've made the date, and there's nothing more to discuss. Having to reschedule is fine, and so is dropping hints at a rich, bustling life beyond the Internet. Tweaking the plan, though, is just second-guessing yourself and makes it seem to your date like it's probably smart to do the same, because you're kind of a basket case.

Five Ways to Blow It on Social Media
Before You Meet in Person

The most accurate social media representation comes from just being yourself. But as we mentioned earlier, sometimes being yourself means being a total disaster. If your self tends to say awful things online that dates will hate, maybe be a different self? You don't need to censor everything, but there are five specific types of statuses to avoid:

- **Vindictive:** "What would it be like if all your exes died in a fire? Not asking for a friend."

- **Cryptic:** "Why does this always happen to me? Do I have a sign on my back? Secret back signs are worse than Hitler."

- **Drunk:** "Maybe the eartg and sun are like fogments if our imagintions and each of us = god of our own dormain?"

- **Inappropriate:** "Yo, does Arbor Day make anyone else wild horny?"

- **Using the word "haters" in any context:** "To all my haters, I can't hear you over the sound of my life being more awesome than yours in every way. Anywayz, you can collect my taxes in hell, IRS."

Exit Interview for an Online Date

So you've decided not to pursue this opportunity. While it's certainly a shame to lose such an obviously qualified candidate, we understand that sometimes these things just don't work out. Please take a few moments to fill out the following questionnaire so that we may continue improving our process and find an ideal match.

- What attracted you to this company in theory that you did not find in practice?
- Did you feel you received enough positive feedback on your performance? The company made it clear several times how much fun it was having.

- Did you seek counsel from an associate when deciding not to pursue this opportunity? Was it Alex? Your friend whose nickname is Hurricane Alex?

- Did the company's benefits package seem inadequate? Because it's totally not.

- What are some areas that need improvement? Be gentle— the company is barely holding it together right now.

- What kind of candidate would not find this company to be, in your terms, "a gaping black hole of need?"

- Would you recommend other prospective candidates? What about the other people in your profile picture? What are their names?

- Have you already accepted another opportunity? Because that is ice cold.

- What would it take to make you reconsider? The company is literally begging here.

CHAPTER 7

Relationships: The Champagne of Compromises

I f you've waded through the knotty thicket of creeps, losers, monsters, dummies, criminals, and empty husks long enough to make a connection with another person...way to go! You've likely salvaged your faith in humanity for long enough not to run into the woods and live in a cave among bears and (fingers crossed) Sasquatch. Not to mention, you *may* be in a relationship.

We say "may" because nowadays it's hard to define what constitutes a relationship. Sixty years ago, things were so simple. A guy got his high school sweetheart pregnant, and if they were religious, they decided they were in love and spent the rest of their lives together deluding themselves into happiness. Or, for same-sex couples, they fled to coastal cities far away from their hometowns, which are run by former high school football heroes. We've all heard the classic American love stories.

Lately, it's grown harder to find that one special person to cling to with terrified intensity until death claims you both, two wrinkled, unfulfilled bags of flesh and guts. But fret not! It's still possible! There's plenty of opportunity to find your soul mate and slowly drain the life out of each other like dueling Texas oil barons. Here's a guide to what to expect from a relationship, starting at the giddy, emotionally unsustainable beginning, and ending at the wine-drunk, voice-mail-leaving conclusion.

The Honeymoon Phase: Literally Too Good to Be True

You've just met someone new, and you don't want to get ahead of yourself, but you really think he or she might be *the one*. Congratulations, you've entered the honeymoon phase! Or, as we prefer to call it, "the golden age of denial." It's a magical time, one that could lay the tracks for a smooth, beautiful relationship. Or, more often, it's a period of exhilarating romance in which each partner tacitly agrees to ignore all the most hateable things about the other and even claims to find those things cute.

During the honeymoon phase, we participate in rituals known as "the casual revealing of our deepest flaws" and "the assurance that your worst qualities are no big deal." But do not be fooled. When a person you've just started dating admits a grievous deficit of character, that does *not* mean "except with you." If your new girlfriend says, "I don't believe in being with one person, so I usually cheat on my boyfriends after, like, three months," then guess what?... You're going to get cheated on in eight weeks. If your new boyfriend admits, "I have a hard time remembering birthdays and names of girlfriends' families because I don't care about other people that much," then don't be surprised when he skips your parents' thirtieth anniversary dinner to rewatch season one of *Bar Rescue* for no particular reason. (Not that you really need a reason. *Bar Rescue*!)

As Chekhov once said: "If you chew with your mouth open on the first date, you'll have a screaming fight about it at a restaurant on Valentine's Day a year later." But don't even try to put the brakes on the honeymoon phase. You can't. The endorphin levels are too high. Instead, just ignore all the red flags as if they were ornaments in a Mao Tse-tung remembrance parade and not an accumulation of hellish, untenable traits that will eventually ruin your life. Stick your head in the sand like an ostrich. Do ostriches mate for life? We have no idea. They probably used to, but now they do SoulCycle and play the field forever like a bunch of flightless Jennifers Aniston.

The Middle Part: Era of Sweatpants

By the time the golden age of denial has ended, you have to decide whether you're sick of each other's naked bodies and taste in movies and just *live* together. Wait. You're not *already living with each other*, are you? If so, put down this book. You're destroying lives at an advanced level. You have graduated from run-of-the-mill blowing it and should probably just move to Miami, start wearing white linen blazers, and pick up a fashionable coke habit. (It goes with *everything*!)

In general, the best and most consistent way to ruin a relationship that's going along smoothly is to base your expectations on television and movie relationships. Just let the relationships you've seen onscreen dictate what you'll be expecting, and react accordingly. Men: Complain about having to go to the ballet.

Women: Withhold sex when he buys the wrong scented soap. Pop culture shows a lot of whirlwind romance and then a lot of fighting over people not doing chores right. You know what they don't show? People doing chores right. The sitcoms we grew up on portrayed the *worst* relationships. Everybody seemed to love Raymond, except for his wife. She fucking hated him.

Spend every waking hour thinking about your relationship, not the person you're in a relationship with. It's an important distinction. Don't spend your time daydreaming about the object of your affection; use those idle hours to assemble a checklist of affection objectives. Are things moving too fast? Not fast enough? Did your friends just get engaged? You should probably be engaged. Did your friends just break up? That's a great idea. Comparing yourselves to others is the perfect way to make sure you always have something to feel anxious about. Spend lots of time with other couples, especially the ones you hate. That way you can feel superior to them *and* learn new things to fight about.

A little insecurity is part of any relationship: the *worst* part. Being jealous and possessive undermines any goodwill you may accrue. An exciting way to erode your lover's trust is picking a friend of his or hers to be suspicious of. Narrow your eyes and shake your head whenever the friend's name is brought up. Insist that there's something you "just don't trust" about him or her. Soon your suspicion will lower you into the bowels of unrestrained madness. Obsess over their friendship. Let it consume you like Moby-Dick (either in terms of Ahab's quest or the sense of literally being eaten by a whale). Just like a boxer, by clinching someone close to you, you can assure that he or she will want to push away.

So if jealousy can erode romance, the ultimate expression of commitment must be an open relationship, right? Wrong! While one in ten open relationships is healthy and lovely, the other 90 percent are excuses to sleep with other people while still giving you the high ground to get mad at your significant other. Most discussions that lead to open relationships go like this:

"I'm going to sleep with other people. Should we break up, or will you pretend you're cool with it?"

"Oh yeah, it's 2015. Of course I'll pretend to be cool with this thing I don't want at all because it seems progressive."

If you are already having troubles, opening the relationship up will cause it to spiral out of control as fast as possible. It's like jumping out of a plane with a garbage bag for a parachute. Yeah, it *looks* like it might work, and you're pretty sure you saw Wesley Snipes do it in a movie once. But it won't work. Not even almost.

"That's Not Funny"

A sense of humor can buoy any relationship, but some topics are generally off-limits unless you're ready for the kind of fight that Eminem and Rihanna write songs about. Try to avoid these verbal land mines:

- Your partner's recent weight gain

- Your partner's likely future weight gain

- Your potential for future sexual congress with a former lover

- The smells of your partner's various family members (unless she brings them up first)

- How unknowingly bad your partner is at something he takes pride in
- The Holocaust (unless he brings it up first)
- Your partner's history of mental illness or drug abuse
- Unironically enjoying *Full House*
- Your partner's death
- The modest number of people sexier than your partner here on vacation in Acapulco
- That thing you agreed you'd never bring up again even though you don't think it's that big a deal

---

Streaming Match: The Drama of Deciding What to Watch

Once you've progressed to the sweatpants-and-ordering-in phase of a relationship, any individual night can be squandered simply deciding what to watch on TV. A night in can be relaxing and regenerating if you spend it wisely. If you don't, you may as well have stayed up until dawn on an acid trip gone sideways.

A quick preemptive note on watching shows together: If you've decided to watch a series as a couple and one of you gets ahead of the other, he or she has committed a breach of trust worse than cheating. You risk being dumped unceremoniously, and found guilty in the court of public opinion. Here are the four worst mistakes couples make while choosing the night's entertainment:

1. Decide who's going to decide.

Both people should defer to the other's taste. You don't really care what you watch, do you? Let your partner decide what you'll spend the evening ignoring each other for. But wait, he doesn't care either. You're now in television purgatory. Stay there as long as you'd like, friend. To paraphrase the Eagles, you can log out of Netflix anytime you like, but you can never leave.

2. Reject your partner's every idea.

No, I don't feel like a whole movie. Ugh, *Grey's Anatomy?* Yes, it has been a while since we've watched a documentary, but does it have to be such a depressing one?

3. Browse aimlessly.

Since none of the initial offerings struck your fancy, meander listlessly through the home screen of HBO GO, On Demand, or, *gasp,* live television listings. Everything looks kind of okay, but the odds are stacked against it actually being okay. Streaming movie services mostly exist to prove that if you've never heard of a movie, it's for a reason. So you end up bouncing back and forth between options, looking for anything you might have missed, like you're trying to solve a murder.

4. Give up.

Netflix has ushered us into a golden age of watching half a movie and never finishing it. And that's fine. If you don't like a thing, forget it. Nothing in the history of entertainment suits your mutual tastes this evening. Let the screen go black, symbolizing the void that constitutes your social life. Lie in bed next to each other and read like it's 1862. Quietly resent your significant other for refusing to watch *Die Hard* on basic cable, starting in the middle.

Breaking (Up) Bad: How to Screw Up Screwing Up

Obviously, not every relationship lasts forever. (Nothing does, not even cold November rain. That's a saying we invented. Sounds badass, right?) Once you've cheated/been cheated on/ fallen out of love/decided the whole concept of love is a sham, it may seem like the worst is over. But fear not, a bad thing can still get worse. A breakup gives you the perfect opportunity to add insult to injury—or, as we should say, "add tofu to a kale salad." In case you're worried that a "conscious uncoupling" (Remember when Chris Martin and Gwyneth Paltrow called their breakup that? Remember when they were married? Remember how fleeting life is?) has achieved its maximum painfulness, just remind yourself that given the emotionally raw state you're in, *almost anything* can make your situation worse.

Keep sleeping together. That helps nothing. Or talk *lots* of trash to mutual friends. That can't *not* backfire! But really, the easiest and worst mistake we make is trying to be friends.

What? How? you may ask. *Friendship is the greatest gift that one person can give to another. How could that be the WORST MISTAKE?* In many ways, you'd be right. As children, we learn lots of songs about the value of friendship. Anyone who doesn't treasure the idea of being friends is either a cat or someone who recently became obsessed with home-brewing beer and can't shut up about it. But while the importance of being friends was drilled into our heads with cartoon shows and songs, we were never taught the nursery rhyme in which Jack and Jill can't even hang out in groups because they keep arguing over whose fault it was that they fell down the hill. And no one bothered to make the animated series *My Little Pony: I Just Need Some Time to Process This! Okay, Steve?* Most good, healthy friendships don't require effort. They just work. So if you're trying to be friends, you're doing something wrong to begin with (the key problem here is the word "trying"). It's like trying to breathe. Either you're drowning or you're making a ridiculous-looking attempt at a thing that should be natural because you got way too high. You can't even think about breathing without starting to do it wrong. You're probably doing it right now. Breathe in. Breathe out. Now you're breathing funny and you have "Machinehead" by Bush stuck in your head.

Unfortunately, during a breakup, not trying can make your life miserable, too. Breakups encourage nature's most destructive form of inertia, the wallow. Wallowing takes your ill feelings, whether they be resentment/self-loathing/fear/loneliness or just plain old spite, and soaks you in them all at once, until your life becomes a bombardment of all the wrong flavors. Your emotional state is a marinade of despair that you can't help but mop up with the bread of anxiety.

Of course, you can wallow for a little while. Pain hurts, despite what Patrick Swayze said in the cinema classic *Road House.* (If you're not a film snob like we are, the quote is: "Pain don't hurt.") One rule of thumb is that you get half the length of your relationship to get over it. We propose taking thrice the length of the relationship. Become an emotional hoarder. Drive away your family and friends with the moldy crate collection of your feelings. Wallowing turns every experience into a grotesque, inside-out version of itself. Is your favorite TV show on? Well, now it's ruined by your constant dismay. Is that song you hate on the radio? Now you *double hate* it. Wallowing is a hangover you give yourself, and it's one that can't be cured with egg sandwiches and Gatorade.

Even the old hangover cure "hair of the dog" (aka drinking) is powerless against your misery. You just cry louder and swear less coherently. Also destructive is the conventional wisdom that "the best way to get over the last person is to get under the next one." Quick tip: Any life advice that includes a sexual position is probably not the most circumspect. Bad sex will make you miss your ex. (If your ex was good at sex, you'll be disappointed. If your ex was bad at sex, it will remind you of him or her. "That's the way Michael always dripped sweat in my eyes and pulled my hair at the wrong moment.") Good sex may ease the pain for a little while, but it's sadness ibuprofen, not a sadness antibiotic.

If you really want to make your breakup complicated, pretend you've gotten over it *superfast*. You'll feel great, but you'll be subject to the judgy looks of friends and family, not to mention passive-aggressive correspondence from your recent ex. (Oh, you like that Facebook picture of the two of us, do you? No. You just wanted me to see that you saw it. *I know your games.*) Remember, you two are now nemeses. Every move you make in regard to one another should be a head game or a reverse, nonhead-game head game. Treat your exes casually. Invite them to your birthday party. Text them when songs remind you of them in non-romantic ways. No one wants to be moved on from, and nothing says, "I've moved on!" like ... well ... moving on. This sounds like the aforementioned "trying to be friends," but it's slightly different. Unlike trying, this is a one-sided effortlessness. And it's totally infuriating and will not go unpunished. So if you're hoping to get over your breakup, you'd better not actually get over it. That will only make it worse.

Just keep waiting until one day when you've both finally grown out of the breakup. Then, and only then, will you be able to meet a wonderful new person, and ruin his or her life, too.

Joe Blew It: A Tale of Two Parties

Bachelor parties are for celebrating a relationship's imminent entry into the "contractual obligation" stage. They can also mark the end of a relationship for any of the groomsmen, if they're not careful enough. Or at least, that's what happened to me.

My friend Andy's bachelor party consisted of a stripper-free visit to the happiest place on earth: Six Flags Great Adventure, in New Jersey. The excursion was not without some of the usual bachelor party trappings, though. Despite the absence of in-person nudity, the TVs in our limo streamed porn on a continuous loop, in case we got pulled over and had to prove to cops that we were super hetero. Our alcohol supply was infinite, with two different kinds of absinthe alone. Perhaps more potent, though, we had pot-laced Rice Krispies treats, a questionable addition to any roller-coastering experience. All told, we had an embarrassment of riches, which perfectly set the stage for the embarrassment of embarrassments to come.

What happened over the next three hours is virtually inde-

scribable, for both lack of memory and absence of dignity. Need-
less to say, alcohol, edibles, and roller coasters do not go together.
Neither do fully grown men and Looney Tunes–costumed Six
Flags entertainers. We laughed like maniacs. We screamed like
children. We got chased all over by security, for a variety of reasons. Only two groomsmen survived the day without passing out
or throwing up on anything, and I was one of them. Once the pot
wore off a little, I felt so confident in my abilities that I began
exchanging texts with my new girlfriend, Meghan.

As it turned out, Meghan was planning some fun of her own
that day. She and a few friends had decided to throw an im-
promptu dinner party at her place, and after a string of texts, she
invited me. The reason I should've declined, though, was the
same reason I eagerly accepted. We'd been going out only about
six weeks. We were still at the tenuous point early in a relationship where it seems as though it could all end on a whim. Or
maybe that's just my experience. In any case, her invite struck
me as an express lane to intimacy. In no way did I consider that
she was maybe just being polite and I was maybe not in the right
head space to show Meghan's friends just what she saw in me.

Later that night, as I began introducing myself with sloppy
high fives, I felt my confidence carry over from Six Flags, where I'd
easily been among the most coherent and well maintained of the
group. What I didn't realize is that going directly from a bachelor
party to a civilized gathering of adults is like going from playing
Little League to playing for the Yankees at Fenway Park in Boston.

I was so wired that I forgot essential social graces, like showing any interest in other people, talking with no food in my
mouth, and not having bright red, bloodshot eyes. The only

thing I did right was to continue not throwing up, and somehow I thought this was enough to blow Meghan away. "What kind of boyfriend leaves a bachelor party to hang out with me and my friends?" she was thinking, in my dumb head. *Um, only the most rad goddamn boyfriend you ever had.*

The next morning, my eyes fluttered open to reveal Meghan's angry face mere inches from mine. The face was oozing repulsion, not just for me, but for its owner's choices. The relationship wasn't over, exactly, but it was the beginning of the end. And probably also the middle. (She dumped me two weeks later.) In the haze of THC and roller coasters, it hadn't occurred to me to just be a guy who has his own life, instead of dropping everything to meet my new girlfriend's friends before she might have been ready for that. I'd gotten just as tangled up in my delusions as the guy at every traditional bachelor party who ends up convinced the stripper is into him. And pretty soon, I would be just as disappointed and alone, but thankfully without any strippers laughing about me.

Fight Scorecard

When you fight, fight to win. Otherwise, how will you know who has the upper hand? Here's how to know whether you came out on top in any squabble:

- If you make the other person cry without yelling: +10 pts.
- If you cry and the other person apologizes: +10 pts.
- If the other person slams a door: +5 pts.
- If you induce the other person to insult your parents: +10 pts.

- Each deep sigh or eye roll you perform: 2 pts.

- Each deep sigh or eye roll you *induce*: 3 pts.

- If the other person says, "We'll talk about this later!":
  +15 pts.

- Threatening to leave somewhere, alone, early: +10 pts.

- Calling the other person's bluff about leaving early:
  +20 pts.

- Successfully bringing up something from the past:
  +10 pts.

- Calling bullshit on the other person for bringing up the
  past: +5 pts.

- Distracting the other person from why they're mad at
  you: +10 pts.

- For every tenth of a second you pronounce the word
  "bullllllllshiiiiit": +1 pt.

- Whisper-screaming: +5 pts.

- Actually screaming: -5 pts.

- Laughing: -15 pts.

- Doing a mocking impression of the other person: -10 pts.

- Saying, "You're acting just like your father/mother!":
  +25 pts.

- Asking the other person if you can finish a goddamn
  sentence: +5 pts.

- Did you end up sleeping on the couch? If yes: -50 pts.

Whoever has more points at the end of the fight wins!

It's that simple. Hold it over your significant other's head
forever. You've earned it.

WELCOME TO THE
WORKING WEAK

CHAPTER 8

Hire Education

The economy has been rebounding, or maybe it hasn't. To be honest, we're not even 100 percent sure what the economy is. Is this book the economy? What about the Oklahoma City Thunder? Pringles? Regardless, unless you're independently wealthy, you need to find some sort of job. And if you are independently wealthy, stop reading this book. It's almost impossible for you to ruin your life. The only chapter rich people might need would be one about doing cocaine while sailing your boat into a thunderstorm. However, for regular folks, a job is both a necessity and a bonanza of blowing it. A real "blownanza." Which, come to think of it, could also be the name for a cocaine thunderstorm disaster.

It seems like only yesterday when women were barely allowed to work at all and men did whatever antiquated job their father did (like town shoe-eater or science guesser). Nowadays, we have so many more options. But where are these jobs? How do we find them? Are there any that pay enough that I could afford to not have roommates?

Who's My Boss?: The Job Search

Many of the people you know probably have jobs. That's how they afford their apartments and stuff. Getting these jobs is a pain in the ass, though. Most of us would take any shortcut to bypass the awful parts of applying for jobs (for example, hiring managers either ignoring your application or printing it out just to play trash-can basketball with it—that's right, they don't even recycle). Here are some of our severely limited usual options.

Craigslist

A Craigslist job posting could provide a completely legitimate employment opportunity. Or it could present a chance for you to get rolled up in a carpet and thrown into the ocean. When exploring listings on Craigslist, be on high alert for a variety of red flags: an interview that takes place at someone's home; a request to arrive slathered in hollandaise sauce; an employer who offers to pick you up in an unmarked van; mandatory toplessness; any listing posted after midnight and before five A.M.; or there is no interview required, but you have to swallow a condom full of unnamed powder on your start date. Truly, Craigslist offers employment with a side of excitement!

Connections

If you went to a prestigious college or share a last name with a skyscraper, chances are there's a job out there with your name on it, perhaps literally. If you weren't so fortunate, you have to work those connections a little harder. You can meet with a headhunter, post your résumé at recruiting sites online, or even use LinkedIn. "What is LinkedIn?" you may ask. The truth is, no one really knows for sure. LinkedIn means something different to everyone. For some of us, it's a place where our ex-boyfriend's brother who sells golf clubs can try to "connect" with us. For others, it's where someone we e-mailed once, five years ago, goes to send us monthly messages we'll never read. We're sure LinkedIn has some practical application for *someone*, but we only ever seem to get weird, unprompted e-mails from it. And we already have jobs. When you're employed, LinkedIn e-mails are like street vendor hot dogs when you're already full—disgusting annoyances that you would resort to without a second thought if you were desperate.

It's Not Who You Know . . . Oh Wait, Yes It Is

The most common way to get a job is through a friend, which works out great for people so charming that everybody wants to hang out with them for eight hours a day. The news of an opening sort of wafts their way like a gentle wave depositing pirate treasure on a lush seashore. The rest of us, though, must go frantically buccaneering toward the gold bullion chest we heard

about in a sea shanty. Instead of directly getting fresh intel about
job leads at a company we'd love to work for, our best hope is
finding out at the same time everybody else does, realizing we
know someone at the gig, and coming forth, hat in hand, to beg
for a mercy referral. It's not so much having the inside track as
having an old-timey handcart on a track running parallel to the
inside track. Proceed with caution.

Not every passing acquaintance you've ever Facebooked is
ideal for approaching about your career; nor can you flat-out
ask him or her for a favor. It would be foolish to Gchat the ex-
boyfriend of your buddy's sister, briefly mention the weather,
and then ambush with: "OH, BY THE WAY, YOU GIVE ME
JOB?" It's more awkward, though, to pretend you care about
this person in any meaningful way rather than just acknowledg-
ing you barely know each other. As you meander toward the
point, your motive slowly reveals itself as an ulterior one. Bury-
ing a request at the end of a bunch of small talk about catching
up and old times is like when congressmen slip sneaky legisla-
tion into bills. Sure, asking about "corporate culture" at the
company is a transparent ruse to get this person to put in a
good word. It sounds less genuine than when a Little League
team that just lost has to say "Good game!" to the team that just
won. But that's how a formality works. When you ask a date
back home to watch a movie, the movie part may or may not
happen, but you're still supposed to talk about *Erin Brockovich*
like you can barely wait to watch Julia Roberts save children
from whales or whatever.

What About Your Friends?

Here are four questions to ask yourself when any friend asks you for a job:

1. Is this good friend also the worst person I know?

Count every nightclub bouncer this friend has ever done karate on, multiply by every time he's made a big production out of splitting a check, and add a thousand points for ever using the words "false flag operation." Just kidding, you already know who your worst friend is without math.

2. Will this friend buy some vague bullshit excuse for not helping?

Explaining why your friend is not a good fit just won't work. Nobody wants to hear that he has painted himself into a corner in which the only options left are NHL mascot and tattoo consultant. Nor do you want your friend to think you're drunk with the power of employability. Your excuse will register as an RSVP in the affirmative for "fighting."

3. Wait, can I just not do anything and say that I did?

Is this the kind of friend who will take your word for it, or does she expect to be looped into an introductory e-mail with the manager? Can you set up a dummy account in the manager's name and neutralize your friend undercover, like a spymaster? And if so, is there a chance that you'll keep up the correspondence long after the position is filled and one day reveal it was you all along, like the end of *You've Got Mail*?

4. Will your boss recognize a halfhearted, due diligence referral for what it is?

Sometimes the way we say something makes it clear

we're really saying something else. Jeremiah Denton was an American prisoner of war in North Korea who famously blinked the word "torture" in Morse code during a televised press conference. If your worst friend keeps asking whether you've helped with her job yet, follow Denton's example and consider moving to North Korea.

Lies, Damn Lies, and Résumés

As you can probably infer from the two accent marks over the *e*'s, "résumé" comes from a French word that means "list of chronological exaggerations." The point of a résumé is to catalog the qualities of the person you wish you were. In other words, it's the online dating profile of the professional world. Employers read that description, hire you, and make you feel like a fraud for tricking them into a relationship.

Obviously, not everything on your résumé can be a lie. If it were, you'd be exposed as a charlatan in your interview and never get the job. Or, you'd be hired by someone very dumb, which sounds enticing (because you can trick and manipulate him or her) but is actually horrible. Working for people you don't respect is like riding public transportation: You can do whatever you want, but if things go badly, there's no one around to help you, and eventually you're going to get sick of the weird urine smells and want to leave.

Not all lies are created equal, so beware when you're touching up your accomplishments not to airbrush your career so heavily that it becomes an unrecognizable caricature.

Okay Things to Lie About:

- Responsibilities at a Job: Why tell a hiring director you brought your boss coffee when you could say that you "secured assets vital to high-level executive functionality on a daily basis"? If you studied the arts in college, chances are you won't get a job in your field, but you can use your creative writing skills to noun-and-verb your way to an interview. It's hardly lying. It's more like *vivid truth amplification.*

- "Special Skills": This is where a white lie goes to become a polished, shiny ivory untruth. Have you ever accidentally opened Microsoft Excel? Congratulations! You are now specially skilled in Microsoft Excel. Do you jog three times a year? *Boom!* You're a "runner."

Things Not to Lie About:

- Anything Google-able: Go hog wild making up awards you won or honors you have received; just don't be dumb enough to name existing accolades. Everyone knows you didn't win the Academy Award for Best Picture in 2006. That was *Crash,* even though whatever you did that year probably deserved it more. Stick to realistic-sounding but unverifiable achievements like your university's "Lamp of Enduring Education" award or your local community's "Swell Lady of the Month" certificate.

Actually, that's pretty much it. Anything that won't come up with a quick Internet search is up to you to fabricate. That includes jobs you held before 1999, things you've done in towns of fewer than 100,000 people, and college clubs and organizations you "founded." Quit living in the past, and start inventing it. Probably no one will check to see whether you started your own newspaper in your hometown as long as you say it folded as soon as you moved away. Go nuts. Because the depressing/liberating truth about it is: No one at this place actually cares about you at all.

Job Interviews: Now I Want to Be Your Dog

Much of what you learn in college boils down to one lesson: how to jump through hoops with Olympic agility. Convince the powers that be that you can deliver the goods and you'll be abusing expense accounts and crushing the dreams of your peers in no time. The other major factor employers consider before hiring you is whether you're the type of person who makes coworkers want to retire from human consciousness. For many of us, it's problems with these so-called soft skills that weigh us down until we sink to the bottom of the sea and our lungs explode.

Right from the moment an interview begins, you're already on the defensive. Someone has looked at your résumé like a baseball card and demanded you show up in person to prove it wasn't forged at some glamour studio in the Mall of America. You must face off against verbal curveballs and judgmental chin music until someone's convinced that not only is your baseball card accurate but you won't prove to be a Michael Vick–type athlete who sounds great on paper, but in person, *whoops,* is a dog murderer.

Your interviewer wants to know all about you, which seems nice enough. Lots of people treat strangers they meet at parties like they have TELL ME ABOUT YOURSELF! spelled out in birthmarks across their faces. The only difference is that if someone doesn't like you at a party, she just walks away and shit-talks you by the cheese plate. If the person interviewing you doesn't approve, you're denied a 401(k) and free postal privileges. It's enough to make anyone a little nervous, but while "never let them see you sweat" is usually a mere turn of phrase, flop sweat on a job interview means you've already nicked the edge of one of those hoops you're meant to jump through, and now you're dangling from it like a paper clip hooked to another paper clip.

Once the pleasantries are out of the way, a segue-proof silence will usher in the interview proper. Your prospective boss talks for a few minutes about the culture and "what we're trying to do around here" while you decide whether to keep your hands clasped in a temple or more of a rhombus situation. You might think lies are what get people in trouble in interviews, and sure, they do—unless *we're* lying about *that*—but the bigger problem is radical honesty. If you're asked about that five-year plan we all definitely update each month by consulting tea leaves and astral charts, you might end up talking about the orphan children you plan on adopting because your husband isn't quite capable, or something equally personal. Now your maybe-boss has pictured you having intercourse *and* crying, creating a swirling vortex of arousal, pity, and orphans through which no job offers can escape. It's basically the opposite of how interviews go in porno movies. (Not hired!)

Once you've answered every question and thrown your own

redundant questions into the mix just to prove you've read the manual, it's time to go. You saucily un-rhombus your fingers and stand up. Hopefully, you weren't sitting cross-legged the whole time, though, because if so, your foot is now asleep and you have to limp across the room like one of those toddlers your husband can't produce, as the person who decides your financial future must run over and open the door so you don't fall down.

Joe Blew It: Disagreeing to Disagree

When actors go on auditions, they're encouraged to make strong choices. Better to go zipping through cornfields like a lunatic than drive safely down the middle of the road. The same does not apply to job interviews, however, when you are not an actor but, rather, a twenty-five-year-old baby-man attempting to play the role of Someone Capable of Performing Basic Tasks.

Back in the pre-Kindle era, I once interviewed for a job as an editorial assistant. The person I hoped to assist was a high-level vet, famous for editing a writer whose spy thrillers are like catnip for dads. Total dadnip. Your dad reads these books and then he rubs his body against a huge scratching post before a one-hour refractory period. Obviously I wanted the job. All that stood in the way was someone currently looking at me like a thing that had just crawled out of a litter box.

In some situations, you find yourself agreeing with every-thing a person says, just to keep the ship sailing smoothly. This was one of those moments. My bobblehead doll impression seemed like the best defense against this stern-faced graybeard, but I think I took it too far. He must have picked up on how all my views on publishing completely mirrored his, and so he threw me a curveball. Out of nowhere, he asked for my general opinion of Thomas Pynchon. I weighed the options for a moment and made the split-second decision not to be wishy-washy. Instead I drove off the middle of the road, deep into the countryside, and did doughnuts atop the battered corpse of a scarecrow.

I told the truth: that Thomas Pynchon was the bane of my literary existence; that despite enjoying many Pynchonesque authors, each time I'd tried reading his books, I got halfway through, felt myself slogging along, and ultimately decided it wasn't worth it to keep going just so I could tell people at bad parties that I'd read the totality of *Gravity's Rainbow*. This was a strong choice, and it turned out to be exactly the wrong one.

"I love Thomas Pynchon," said the editor, thus editing me out of his future. "I've read all of his books—every word. He's... not for everybody."

A puzzled expression played across his face, as though he couldn't fathom how a thing such as me had oozed into his office. Then we just stared at each other for about the length of three Pynchon books, until he said they'd let me know.

I didn't end up getting the job, but at least I was living what Oprah might call an authentic literary existence.

"See You Around . . . Every Day for Eight Hours"

So you've left the interview, and you thought it went great. Maybe it went so well that you even told some friends about it. You were really *vibing*, and you felt a *connection*, and you don't want to sound crazy, but you think this might be *the one that sticks*.

Does any of this sound familiar? If so, it's probably because these are the same lies that you tell yourself after a decent first date. You're hopeful, you feel like you presented yourself well, and you managed to hide any overt indications of your physical arousal the whole time. Well played!

Much like a first date, an interview leaves you with lingering questions: Did they really like me or were they leading me on? Why do I get the feeling they'd take back the last person who did the job if they came waltzing through the door? And, most important: How soon is too soon to follow up? With employment, like romance, you want to make sure you appear interested but not desperate, available but not desperate, and motivated but not desperate. This is a hard balance to strike, because you probably are desperate. Plus, in a professional setting, you are bound by the constraints of . . . you know . . . professionalism. You can't wait a week and then shoot off a casual text like: "so great to meet you lets do it again soon lol." First of all, most business places are into punctuation and capitalization. Second, you can't just text prospective employers. They still have landlines, like our parents all do for some reason.

So how do you reach out, and how soon?

You *could* call to follow up, but it's likely you'll end up talking to an assistant or leaving a message. The more phone calls that go back and forth, the weightier the eventual communication needs to be. Even if it's just a simple attempt to catch up with a friend, if you leave each other more than five messages combined, one of you basically has to tell the other one that you are pregnant or moving to Germany. So feel free to pick up the phone if you're interested in a high-anxiety give-and-take that will likely end with: "Oh, uhhh...I don't know...we'll make some kind of decision in a week or so. Why did you call six thousand times to ask me?"

Your best bet is to send an e-mail. E-mail has numerous benefits over calls, handwritten letters, and the dreaded face-to-face contact. First of all, you can control exactly what you say, and you won't get a spontaneous response that will fluster or confuse you. E-mail is also easy to respond to. Most people can do it from their phones. So you're giving yourself the best chance of getting a speedy reply. Most important, when the prospective employer answers you, there's no pressure to take in the response immediately. Wait a couple of hours. Sober up, you unemployed degenerate. Then write back. Here is a sample e-mail that captures the necessary tone and content of a professional interview follow-up. (Feel free to change the words so it's in your "voice" and your employer won't know you're getting your info from this wildly famous and successful book that they definitely know intimately.)

Dear [Name of Person Who Interviewed You],

Thanks so much for taking the time to have me in for an interview. It was a pleasure[1] learning more about you and your company. Whatever bullshit you do[2] feels like a great fit for me, and I'm curious as to your timetable for choosing a candidate. Your company is a top choice on my list of places to work, but if you've decided to move in a

---

1 A lie.
2 Substitute company's specific bullshit.

different direction, I'd like to know so I can pursue one of my other options.[3] Hope to hear from you soon!

Best,[4]

[Your Name]

Take This Job and Shove It into Your Skill Set

If you manage to skate through the torturous interview process without blowing it, congratulations, you're a working stiff now. You'll find snacks inside the pantry next to some Bruce Springsteen songs written specifically about you. Everything else you need, though, you'll learn in the phase known as "onboarding," which is pretty much the same as getting assimilated into the Borg on *Star Trek*—only with a trayful of Mediterranean wraps instead of a violent injection of nanoprobes.

Apparently, you can't just fart your way through figuring out how stuff works at a job anymore. Instead, you're assigned a buddy à la the first day at a new school, and this person helps you quickly prove your worth as human capital. Sweet, sweet human capital. Too bad your middle school self can't see you now and rest assured that all those atomic nurples will be worth it someday. Here are some ways you might end up shattering young-you's dreams while starting out at a new company:

- Find out who the most capable person is and outsynergize him or her the first day.

---

3 Technically not a lie even if you don't have any offers. Homelessness and a life of crime are both technically "options."

4 A power move. Everyone knows "Best" is code for "Go screw yourself."

- Break the tension of introductions by asking how much money everyone makes.
- Immediately seek clarification on the rules about marrying a coworker.
- Learn which e-mails you can get away with not answering by not answering any at all during your first fiscal quarter.
- Delete random files from the shared drive, just to feel something.
- Ask everybody who they think is the Ringo of the office.
- Whenever you see two or more people laughing, ask what they're laughing about. When they attempt to answer, say, "I don't get it," and start crying.
- Pick one person to ask every single question that comes up, each time presenting him or her with a tiny noose and saying, "Now I'm showing *you* the ropes!"
- Ask your superior about the organization's brand and professional culture so you can align your performance with institutional expectations and ramp up to productivity—then, when he or she starts talking, mention that there's a Japanese serpent ghost circling the room and run for dear life.
- Burn your badge laminate every day, like a cop who's seen too much shit, until they take a photo of you that doesn't look like a celebrity mug shot.

CHAPTER 9

Taking Care of Business

One of the best feelings ever, besides holding your baby for the first time or smiting your enemies, is accepting your dream job offer. We hope to do all three at the same time someday, if we ever give birth just as Justin Timberlake is finally brought to justice and we're promoted to chief executive of Meeting New Kittens. Unfortunately, the glory of earning that new job title tends to wear off before the ink on the contract even dries. What, you didn't sign any contract because nobody does that anymore? Doesn't matter. Stop interrupting.

That burning feeling you had when you wanted the job so badly rarely stays very long after you're hired. Now there's just the day-in, day-out reality of the work itself. (Even meeting new kittens can become a total grind with enough repetition and insufficient fluffiness.) And the whole time you're struggling not to get bored with your job, you also need to prove yourself worthy of promotion to a team you're gradually losing respect for. It may be difficult to convince less talented people that your vision is worth taking seriously, but it's not impossible. After all, in the land of the blind, the man who lies about having one eye is king.

There's just one problem: you. As we've established before, you are your own worst enemy. (Other than Justin Timberlake. He knows what he did.) Your tendency to screw up while going to a party or talking to your boyfriend's parents doesn't just spontaneously combust like vampires in the sun once you set foot in the office. Nope. It follows you to your desk, looks at videos of unlikely animal friendships for twenty minutes, and gets to work.

Absence Makes the Heart . . . Do Something

The greatest thing about a job is not being there. But unlike in high school, where your "permanent record" is largely a myth used to scare you into showing up and behaving, missing work has consequences. At some jobs, they can refuse to pay you if you don't come in, which seems unfair but is true. If you spend enough time not at work, they'll fire you and find someone they can manipulate into coming in more frequently and dressing snazzier.

Arriving at work late and leaving early are the simplest ways to carve out a few extra seconds of freedom, but, unfortunately, they're the most frowned upon. It's a shame. So many places we have to go are open only during "business hours," which are (*duh!*) the hours you, also, are doing business. How are you supposed to go to the doctor or get a good deal at a buffet if you're always at work? We get sick days and vacation days, but usually you can't break those down by the minute. Sometimes you're half an hour behind because you got stuck watching compilation videos of NBA players missing dunks, and that's not okay for some reason, but it's perfectly fine for Craig from Human Resources to take his kids to Disney World for a *whole week*? Whatever! If you *are* running late, though, don't dare show up with a coffee, or everyone will act like you stopped at a casino on the way to a funeral.

If you have to leave the office early, which you may if you have children or pets or friends or dreams, leave quickly and without a trace. With e-mail at your fingertips constantly, you can stay in the loop and pretend to be present. Everyone will assume you're pooping. On your way out, act like you're heading to the break room, and keep walking to your ill-gotten freedom like Kevin Spacey at the end of *The Usual Suspects*. (Oh, have you not seen that movie? Well, here's a hard truth: You weren't going to, so suck it up.) Anyway, this advice mostly applies if you have an office job. If you work in service, construction, or education, you can't just sneak away. (Well, you can, but people will notice.) Unfortunately, this reduces your flexibility. On the other hand, you're less of a faceless cog in the machine of capitalism, so that's something to celebrate, right?

In the modern age, taking a sick day is both easier and more complicated than it used to be. With text messaging and e-mail, you no longer have to fake-cough when leaving a message on an answering machine to play up how unhealthy you are. ("Hey old men, what's an answering machine?" Don't worry about it.) Nowadays, communicating that you may have something communicable is a matter of timing and etiquette. You want to give your employer enough time to plan for your absence if you can, but don't provide too much notice, or it'll be obvious you're faking. A text message five minutes before your shift begins is rude. But so is e-mailing on a Monday: "I'm going to be sick on Friday." Clearly, you're either fabricating an illness or shot-calling a Thirsty Thursday–related hangover, Babe Ruth style.

Requesting vacation time, on the other hand, must be done well in advance, and even then it is a minefield of political entanglements the likes of which started World War I. Unless you work at a place that's closed over major holidays (public schools, the post office, video stores… which are closed every day forever now), those days will be picked over by your boss, any worker who's been there longer than you, and whoever makes the vacation schedule. If you don't weasel your way into the good graces of those in charge, you're going to end up covering Easter, the Fourth of July, and Bastille Day while your lucky coworkers get to gorge on chocolate eggs, set off explosives, and storm French castles.

Some jobs let you use sick time and vacation time interchangeably. That way, you won't be penalized with extra workdays for going through a year without succumbing to the bug that ravaged your office like a horrific puke fire. This arrangement also gives you the benefit of getting paid even if you *did* get sneezed on by the one guy you work with who *doesn't know* to do that into your elbow so no one else gets sick and have to miss an extra few days, assuming of course that you didn't plan any recreational time away from your job all year. Even between sick days and vacation time, chances are you won't have a satisfying amount of time off. It seems like you should just be able to not show up and not get paid whenever you want, but *nooooooo*. It's likely that you need the money. Why else would you even have a job? Are you a rich person trying to relate to "normies"? An alien trying to assimilate into human life? Taking time off of work is a "damned if you do/damned if you don't" paradox. If you do it too much, you lose your job. But if you don't do it enough, you're at your job an awful lot. And on the off-chance you do take off for a fun-filled day of brunch and museum visits, you will feel haunted by guilt and spend the day hearing phantom e-mail alerts.

Meetings: No Wrong Answers, Just Wrong You

Everybody wants a seat at the table: middle managers shut out of the executive level, partygoers playing musical chairs, pets who think they're people, and other big fans of tables. It's especially apparent at meetings, though, where some of the team always ends up sitting on a nearby countertop, or on the floor like common street trash. So when you sit at the table, you're making a statement: "I belong here. I will not scooch over for Gary from Marketing." The only catch is that now you have to prove you do belong. You have to contribute enough that your presence essentially says, "Fucking take *that*, Gary!"

Meetings are all about getting together with your colleagues in person to figure out which decisions one of you will later make alone. Each meeting is a bustling flea market of placeholder ideas that range from almost good enough to future inside joke. Even though these ideas will all be discarded in favor of whatever the decider's personal Iago likes, you still have to throw some out there. Making even one semi-intelligible comment gets you points on the board. Nobody can say you weren't there now. It's also just an opportunity for some regular old face time with those who control your corporate destiny. Unfortunately, this face time may include more mouth time than brain time, turning it into a power hour of anatomical calamity.

Here are some things you could do that are worse than just being silent room-meat:

Tap Dancing

This is when you have nothing to say but still keep yammering on with the clacking fury of Sammy Davis Jr.'s Capezios. Rambling may have been the ideal lifestyle for country-western musicians of yore, but that's why so many are now late-stage alcoholics with only dead plants and nicotine patches for company.

Devil's Advocating

"Allow me to play devil's advocate" is a thinly veiled way of saying, "Here's why your shitty idea sucks." When your only contribution to a meeting is shooting down someone's idea, it's even less productive than shuffling deck chairs on the *Titanic*. It's like critiquing the people doing that for shuffling too slowly.

Turd Polishing

You can't "eureka" a "duh." That's when you remix some fairly obvious concept with dumb buzzwords (like "eurekduh") and act like you just invented the Bible.

You didn't do that, though. You invented nothing. You didn't even invent the King James Bible, which is, in all fairness, the most successful remix of all time.

Umming Up Short

Sometimes you start talking with only a vague notion of a point, the preferred style of audiences during the Q&A portion of any event. After a while, though, your point gets more and more muddled, and you panic. That's when the *um*s spill out of your mouth like a bushel basket of banana peels your tongue tripped over. Losing your train of thought in a meeting is the quietest train wreck of all; the little train wreck that could.

Until recently, the only distractions during meetings were the weirdly revealing doodles your coworkers made when they didn't realize they were being observed. (Who knew Cynthia could draw so many guillotines with such realistic shading?) Now, of course, we have to pretend not to have the most entertaining device in the world right there in our pockets and that we wouldn't rather be dicking around on our phones during a lull ("lull" is Norwegian for "meeting").

The best you can do is look at your phone briefly while scrunching your face into a mask of confusion, as though you need to get to the bottom of something right now, for the sake of everyone at this table and beyond. If you don't have that bomb-defusing look while brazenly finger swiping, everybody notices and judges you for it. Always. Even when the meeting finally descends into a prolonged side conversation about *Antiques*

Roadshow between whoever's in charge and one other person, even though everybody has to pee but it'd be weird to leave so close to the end—even then, people still notice your phone's been out for longer than it takes to read a text message, and they silently start kicking around mean nicknames for you.

Reply "Aww": The Trials and Tribulations of Work E-mail

Work e-mails typically start off with a message of hope.

- *Hope* all's well! Specifically, I hope your parents are okay.
- *Hoping* to catch you! Tried your phone but then I remembered phones are phones.
- *Hope* you had a great weekend! If not, I hope you're not haunted at night by regret.

Hope springs eternal in work e-mails, because a lot can go wrong with them. Unlike meetings, where any botched move leaves only a faint residue in coworkers' memories, work e-mails spread a bread crumb trail of your incompetence across the Internet. Every typo, every exchange that got overheated; they've all been logged, and they're available as blackmail. You have to hope you don't make any mistakes, and if you do, you have to hope nobody notices, and then if you're fired, you have to hope there are openings for a new job—one that doesn't require e-mail, like a fighter pilot or something.

Between the slippery AutoFill in the address field and you being deeply fallible, there's always a chance you'll send an e-mail *about* a person *to* that person. Historically, accidental e-mails are never flattering. Or at least they're never flattering in a way that isn't sexual and gross. In fact, you should be very suspicious upon receiving an e-mail intended for Keith that glowingly references your business acumen or Borat impression. What's more likely to happen is that you'll write an e-mail about why Keith is kind of a tool and accidentally send it to Keith himself. All you can really do in that situation is to get out in front of your blunder with one of the following excuses:

- It's an office meme. Now *you* pretend to tell someone he's the worst, and pay it forward.
- Wrong Keith. So many Keiths!
- It was a digital trust fall exercise—you did not pass.
- The office has been compromised. Pretend you never read that e-mail. *We've never even spoken.*
- Sentient computers. The robot uprising is real and it's happening now, and it starts with you.
- We were hacked by North Korea. Will they never learn?
- G-g-g-g-g-g-ghost e-mail!
- Temporary insanity. I'm going through some stuff.

What calls for more explanation than sending the wrong e-mail to the wrong person is sending the wrong e-mail to a hundred wrong persons at once. The REPLY ALL option was invented for efficiency, but in the long run it takes up even more time since you now have to roundhouse kick your computer in the face whenever someone responds to a mass message with "K, thanks!" Other times, a company-wide health-care update erupts into open mike night at the Chuckle Bucket, as people pile on zingers they decided absolutely had to be seen by others. ("Blood drive? Who am I, Dracula?")

But these people all *meant* to respond to everyone, misguided as that seems. The real danger comes when you veer off the main e-mail avenue into the dark, shady backstreets—replying to one person or forwarding to someone else—and then go back to the original thread. Now there are two separate e-mail threads in play, both with the same subject line. You're basically living parallel lives. In one, you're a savvy office worker getting stuff done, and in the other, you're the wisecracking sidekick who tells it like it is. But when these two trade places, anything can happen! "Anything," of course, being you accidentally replying to the wrong thread. Now your two worlds have collided in a greater identity crisis than your college gothabilly phase but just as mortifying. There's only one thing left to do: blame it on Keith.

The Customer Is Always . . . There

Whether you're a server at a chain seafood restaurant, a birthday party clown, or a life insurance salesperson, the people who keep you in business are also the people who make you want to run away into the woods. (If you are a lumberjack, we assume your lumberjacking clients make you want to rejoin urban society.) This happens because even though you are the expert who does your job every day of the week, your customers are often amateurs who make the same simple mistakes and asinine demands as every other customer you serve, over and over like in *Groundhog Day*. After dealing with customers as a professional, you become intimately familiar with the little phrases that might ruin an employee's day:

"Can you check again though?"

"Uhhh, you always *used to* do that here." [You *never* did.]

[Customer, after looking at a menu that says NO SUBSTITUTIONS.] "Okay, but can I make a substitution?"

"Is there a manager here I can speak with?"

"Is there *anyone* else I can talk to about this?"

"How long have you been working here?"

"But the Web site said I can pay in bitcoin."

"Are you sure that's the best you can do?"

"I never had to do that before." [They *always* had to do that before.]

"Can you make an exception this *one* time?"

"Haven't you ever heard 'the customer is always right'?"

"I'm going to write a Yelp review about this."

Performance Review Anxiety

The performance review was invented in 1967 when a guy named Frank Duffy responded to one of those HOW'S MY DRIVING? bumper stickers that truckers have. Duffy called up the 800 number listed, said nothing about trucks or driving, but complimented the bumper sticker itself for being "groovy as balls." Another classic American creation story.

All these years later, the tradition lives on. Performance reviews are either where you explain why an enormous salary increase will save the company or where you beg not to get fired for gross negligence. It all depends on what kind of year you've had, how the company's doing, and the way you plead your case. That's right—performance reviews are like trials in which you defend the privilege of keeping your job. Not going to the review at all is called "putting the system on trial," and it's what James Dean would have done.

The way most people embarrass themselves in a performance review is by making an emotional plea rather than citing concrete data. An employee under review might claim he deserves a promotion because of what he went through in the war (any war, even one with a neighbor over Wi-Fi passwords). Either that or he might cite seniority. While that may have worked during the 1950s, when management was largely drunk or hopped up on goofballs, these days job loyalty is considered a sign of being too lazy or incompetent to get a better job. All your boss sees in either scenario is you saying "Me wantee!" while wearing a baby bonnet and a poopy diaper, and that's how you'll always look henceforth.

Of course, going the other way might not go over any better. If you walk in with reams of data about deliverables met and how much your coworkers make and what Macaulay Culkin got paid for *Home Alone 2: Lost in New York*, your supervisor might be impressed. She might also tell you to calm down. Acting entitled to a promotion because of your market value can rub people the wrong way. It's like demanding a date with the prom queen on the strength of having the same grades as her boyfriend. Your research shows nothing about whether people in similar positions who are earning your target salary got there by being dicks about it.

Beyond mapping out your future with the company, or perhaps your future catching up on video games and pot, the performance review is also a chance to evaluate your boss. Oh, how the tables have turned! Except for how they haven't turned at all! This is no anonymous survey, so any criticism should be served as lightly as angel hair pasta atop a bed of cotton swabs. Maybe complain about how her judgment is *too* evenhanded, or that it seems suspicious how much animals and babies like her. Once your boss seems pleased, the performance review is over. Now bang your fist against the desk like a gavel and moonwalk out of the room.

Blowing the Job

We all know how we'd quit our jobs in a perfect world. You've probably fantasized about it more frequently and in greater detail than you've imagined your wedding or what you'd say if you ever met George Clooney in person. (FYI, we'd go with: "Looks like the wild Cloondog has finally been tamed. Awoooooo!") You've envisioned whom you'd flip off, some colorful phrases you'd include in your letter of resignation, and the parade of coworkers who would hoist you onto their shoulders in solidarity and carry you out of the building (or away from the archaeology site, or out of the private jet you fly, or far from the field where you pick oranges).

In reality, you never get to quit the way you've imagined. The reasons are diverse: You lose your nerve, or you don't have access to enough bees to really shake shit up, but usually it comes down to reality: *You're going to need another job.* So even if the place you're leaving is a literal crap-shoveling factory where your boss is a scorpion who is on fire, you can't storm out the way you want because you can't leave a yawning chasm in your work history. (Why did you stay at the crap-shoveling factory for four years anyway? Were you waiting for a promotion to head crap shoveler, aka craptain?)

Dream Quitting Scenario: You stand on your desk and clear your throat. "Attention, losers. I'm out of here and never coming back. Consider this my two weeks' notice, effective immediately because y'all are 'too weak' to stop me from leaving." You toss your employee ID into your wastebasket, flip a lighter open, and set it on fire. The coworkers you like cheer. The coworkers you hate cower. Your boss emerges from his or her office.

"I was wrong about you," your boss says, handing you a wad of untaxed cash. "You are a hero and a champion."

You take the money without saying a word and walk away, wastebasket still flaming. A flock of doves emerges behind you, seemingly out of nowhere.

The next week you return just to throw eggs at your old workplace while leaning out the side of your new private helicopter.

Actual Quitting Scenario: You write a polite letter to your boss so you can still use him or her as a reference. You tell a few coworkers you're leaving and avoid eye contact with everyone else on the way out. If you're lucky, there's a cake from a grocery store.

If you're fired from your job, you get a little more leeway to behave badly. It's the same premise that states when you get dumped, you can openly shit-talk your ex and sleep around like it's your last week on earth. The bridge has already been burned. You're just peeing into the body of water where it used to be. Unfortunately, when you're fired, it's a lot harder to explain to your friends/family/future employers why you're so up-to-date on daytime talk shows and how come you bought everyone gas station burritos for their birthdays.

If you're very lucky, you can live the dream of being laid off. The ego hit of an employer telling you they "need some time apart to work on themselves" is easily salved by the joy of collecting unemployment while maintaining the moral high ground... aka everyone's fantasy job.

CHAPTER 10

Your Coworkers: Who Are These People?

O nce you've got a handle on the important new job details—finding your preferred bathroom stall with the "comfortable" toilet and locating a safe space for crying on the sly, often the same place—you start to grow curious about your coworkers. You begin to ask yourself, "Who the hell are these people that I see more than my friends and blood relatives?" It's a reasonable impulse. You're stuck in a room full of strangers. What if one is secretly a murderer? Or secretly trying to convert you to another religion? Or secretly really into CrossFit? (Just kidding—no one who is into CrossFit keeps that a secret.) But here's the meta-secret about these secrets: They don't matter. You may become friends with some of these people and see them outside the workplace. You may not. What's more important than most of your colleagues' actual personalities is which workplace arche-type they embody. Every coworker fits a basic type as old as work itself. (Even back when the only job available was the world's oldest profession, there was probably still a gossip in most brothels.) So get to know your fellow employees if you want, but chances are, you've met them all before.

Every Coworker You'll Ever Have

The Social Director

Description: The Social Director loves planning group activities for the office, from happy hours to softball leagues. Social Directors are maybe too into it, though. Like, what kind of life are they avoiding at home? How hollow or terrifying is their existence outside the office? Honestly, who cares? First round's on them!

Typical Quote: "Be there or be square!"

"Cool" Boss

Description: Cool Boss wants you to know that he or she is just like you. Cool Boss doesn't like wearing stuffy suits. Cool Boss isn't hung up on "titles" or "company policy." Except Cool Boss gets paid way more than you and can break rules with impunity while you tiptoe around making sure that Cool Boss's Hard-ass Boss isn't there to bust you.

Typical Quote: "Have you read *Outliers*? I think you'd really dig that shizz."

The Danny Glover

Description: The Danny Glover isn't necessarily a man, or black, or named Danny. The Danny Glover is anyone whose overall vibe is "getting too old for this shit." Danny Glover types complain about changes in technology. They complain about changes in protocol. They complain about *you.* Sometimes they come through when you need them to. But usually they're just pissing and moaning when you need to get work done. (The Danny Glover's nemesis is the Early Adapter, the one with the calendar in the cloud and the standing desk and a hologram butler.)

Typical Quote: "I guess that's *another* password I need to remember."

Oversharer

Description: Yes, we ask each other how we're doing in the office. None of us are monsters. Except the Oversharer, who uses a pleasantry as an excuse to launch into an in-depth monologue full of details that most of us wouldn't even admit to our therapists. If there are any Oversharers reading this right now, just know three things: 1) No one wants to see more than one picture of your vacation. 2) The details about your love life are either making us jealous or bumming us out. 3) *Yes,* you should get that rash checked out, and you didn't need to describe it to us first.

Typical Quote: "Have a good weekend! I'll be spending mine alone again!"

Charlie Brownnoser

Description: The Brownnoser isn't always the best employee, but he or she always seems like the best employee. Brownnosers refill the coffeepot. They hand in their paperwork on time. They do all the little things that endear them to bosses, even if they're as smart as a Ziploc bag full of pudding.

Typical Quote: "Of course I can stay late!"

Office Comedian

Description: The Office Comedian should really be called the Office Racist or Office Sexual Harasser. Since Office Comedians laugh after everything they say, maybe Office Sociopath is more apt. We'll say "Comedian" because that's who they think they are.

Typical Quote: "What? Too soon?"

Gym Rat

Description: We all struggle with how to balance work, our social lives, and our health. Not the Gym Rat. He frequently uses work facilities to change into and out of workout clothes, making the rest of us feel like total slobs. Not cool, Gym Rat. Colleagues' workout regimens should be like their sex lives: We don't care what you do on your own time; just don't bring it into the office, and for goodness' sake, shower afterward.

Typical Quote: "Anyone in for a fun run this Sunday at dawn? I'll bring the Clif Bars!"

Swamped Thing (Busy Guy/Gal)

Description: The Swamped Thing is always too preoccupied with work to chat or help you with a project. Swamped Things answer your e-mails only after an immense amount of prompting. And as soon as you are locked into a project, they want to drain minutes out of your day with some very pressing issue that cannot wait. Everything the Swamped Thing is doing is the most important thing. Everyone else's work, in his or her eyes, is essentially mini-golf or paddleboating.

Typical Quote: "Auto-Reply: It may be a while before I get to your e-mail, but that doesn't mean it's not important to me."

Guy Who Tells It Like It Is

Description: The Guy Who Tells It Like It Is is exactly like the Office Comedian except not even pretending to be kidding.

Typical Quote: "I'm just saying what everyone here is thinking."

Weird IT Guy

Description: Not every information technology guy is weird, but everyone this weird is an IT Guy. Weird IT Guy combines a bunch of other tropes into one superstrange hoodie-clad body. There are the long-winded personal revelations you have no interest in. The jokes that are only recognizable as jokes because of the uncomfortable pause after them. The constant vibe of having somewhere more important to be. It's like Weird IT Guy learned how to be human by taking the worst qualities of everyone else in the office and combining them. The only difference is, you really need the IT guy. So you listen to him talk about LARPing because who else is going to reset your network ID?

Typical Quote: [*snicker*] "Are you sure it's plugged in??"

Oh, the Places You'll Get Stuck!

The most confining places in an office can be the ones most built for motion: the elevators we ride, the hallways we walk, and the restrooms we do bowel acrobatics within, despite being millimeters away from people whose children we've met at an off-site family event. What these places all have in common is that the less populated, the better, and if you eat food inside any of them, then you're definitely a serial killer.

No Thanks, I'll Take My Chances Jumping out the Window

It's impossible for a person to resist pressing the button for an elevator they've just arrived at, despite the fact that you were waiting there before and obviously already did that. Nine times out of ten, it's a reflex. That tenth time, though, this person thinks you don't know how buttons work and that you were standing around doing button incantations instead. Just in case, be sure to give this person a withering look right before you both enter a man-size dumbwaiter together. Once inside, you might want to hit the CLOSE DOOR button a hundred times, to prove you know button pushing after all, and to get this over faster. That's about when someone else will walk in, as you're feverishly pressing a button meant to keep that person out. Now you've been caught red-handed in the crime of elevator jacking, the second-worst crime to hold that title.

The dreaded metal rectangle is no less awkward in motion. We've all heard of an "elevator pitch," so named for the decibel level your screams reach when someone starts talking to you inside an elevator. It's because nothing worth hearing has ever been said inside one. Something about the possibility of being trapped in a tiny box forever seems like maybe you should conserve your words for the eventual debate about whom to eat first (the one time you *should* eat anything in there).

When two coworkers get into an elevator, both wearing headphones, they do a split-second scan of each other's faces. "Please don't make me take off my headphones," these faces seem to say. "K Ci and JoJo are really hitting the spot right now, and if anything, I wish I knew *less* about you." But both are terrified of seeming rude, so it's time for talking. Hopefully this exchange provides an audio buffer for the length of the ride to drown out the low hum of mutual indifference. If there isn't a natural tapering off to the conversation by the time they get to their floor, though, the two must idle in the lobby, winding down. Right before it becomes clear that they're headed to the same hallway and collapse into a spasm of full-body sobs.

The Hellish Ways of Hallways

Office hallways are like bustling roads in a disaster movie you are *not* the star of. Instead, you're a human obstacle. Pre-roadkill. Someone is always speed walking behind you down a narrow hall, footsteps nearly syncing up with "Flight of the Valkyries." Side-by-side duos barrel toward you, as the conversation they started on an elevator strains into postverbal gibberish. They might make a halfhearted gesture of getting out of the way, but most of the time you just have to give in and move over or body-check one of them and claim involuntary hockey instincts.

By now, everyone has been an unwilling participant in the hallway dance. It's when two people from opposing sides of a building swerve to avoid impact, but each keeps aiming where the other is headed, like meat magnets. Both parties smile at first and kind of lean into the dorky choreography. "Are we really doing this? Haha, okay!" But when neither makes a big move, both begin doing it *for real*. Little do they know that the two people who first did this dance in the late-1800s Reconstructionist South ended up fighting to the death with crude weapons fashioned out of protractors and an abacus. Their restless office wraiths still linger in modern hallways, possessing those who don't escape lockstep fast enough. Some say office workers will continue reliving this ancient battle until the enchantment is finally broken by true love's kiss.

Just passing someone in a sufficiently wide hall is not without its problems either. Once you see a coworker coming toward you, there's a decision to make. Do you acknowledge this person now and just pretend something amazing is happening on your phone as you get closer? Do you avert your gaze until the last possible second and pretend to be surprised? Or do you start snapping your fingers rhythmically like in *West Side Story*? Either way, you're going to have to try some Office Hallway Faces and feel gross about them. Here are the most common variations in descending order of friendliness:

The High School Yearbook Photo

Looks like: Head swiveled as though a photographer were dangling a plush birdie just out of frame, naive smile full of hope for the future.

Means: "This is so us, meeting like this."

The Folksy Lawyer

Looks like: An overly familiar, shit-eating grin.

Means: "Wherever you go, there you are, but especially in this hallway, amirite?"

The Sorry Senator

Looks like: Lower lip sucked in, cheeks puffed out; a politician's face at a press conference after getting caught sexting an intern.

Means: "I think we can all agree that this is a disappointing turn of events."

Skybrows

Looks like: A smile so strained, the eyebrows above are flying away into heaven.

Means: "Didn't expect to see you here, and I won't expect it next time either. Expectations are for psychics and the first groundhog of spring."

The Silent Scream

Looks like: Barely contained panic; a rookie mortician seeing his first thresher accident.

Means: "Oh no, it's you! How can this even be? Stay in your area!"

The Snub

Looks like: Blank expression, eyes dead ahead, chin raised in determination.

Means: "I either hate you for no reason or I hate that we hooked up one time and now still have to see each other more often than a retired married couple.

Let's All Go to the Bathroom Together, Like a Creepy Family

Do space aliens have office restrooms? It's a question that has haunted scientific minds for centuries. What would these evolved beings think of us entering tiny chambers to do loud, echoey toilet business, only to emerge in a trench coat of farts, coming face-to-face with our bosses? They probably look upon us the same way that new parents view their infant children when they have dirty diapers: with sympathy. If those babies knew what was waiting in the bathrooms of their future offices, though, they'd throw even more of a shit fit. Then again, if they *can* see that far ahead, perhaps those babies can also see what alien bathrooms look like, and let us know.

Let's start with the noise. The relief sounds people make in public bathrooms ironically fill others with a discomfort from which they may never find release. Nobody should have to hear the shoved doors and slammed seats of someone else's four-alarm stomach emergency—but it happens every day. Any talk of the quarterly report while lined up, urinal-side, like pigs at a trough, is punctuated by a symphony of bathroom sounds—including at least one loud *bleep-blorp* from the toileter who forgot to mute *Angry Birds*. You just can't neutralize that kind of background noise with verbal Febreze. Talking in a work bathroom when you're not alone sounds like a less elegant Weird Al parody of conversation.

Perhaps the most awkward part of using the bathroom at work is trying to preserve anonymity. If you walk past a stall and make door-slit eye contact with whoever's inside, that person gets Medusa'd into a toilet gargoyle in both of your memories. The stakes are just that high when pants are low. Fleeing a stall without anyone seeing you feels like getting away with murder, and sometimes there's almost as much planning involved. If an ad sales rep walks in and starts brushing his teeth just as you were about to make your getaway, you now have to stay in the stall until he's done, suppressing all your questions about why he's doing that. (Seriously, why? Is he planning to propose marriage during the budget review?)

The flip side, of course, is when you're washing up, and someone you know walks in. The sight of that stall door closing is the green light that lets you know to leave, right away, or else become super familiar with your work buddy's *personal brand*.

Your Workspace: Where the Magic Happens (the Magic of Being Exasperated)

Some employees strive to be known by all, like anthropomorphic books hurling themselves at nearby eyeballs. Others want to be impenetrable sphinxes. The big cosmic joke is that everybody has to share the same space no matter which way they're inclined. The first group turns their cubicles into real-life Facebook walls, appointing every inch with maximum personal data. The second group's only decorations are the bits of sandwich toppings wedged into their keyboard. Weirdly, anyone who's that boring paradoxically invites suspicion. People walk past their desks that much slower just to see what dark secrets their Web-browsing habits reveal.

But people will do that no matter what! When you're on the clock, sneaking behind someone looking at their furries-only online dating profile gives off the premium rush of a crack hit, with no repercussions. If someone accused you of stealing a peek as he feverishly closed out a tab, *he'd* be the weirdo. This obsession with others' secrets may push us incrementally closer to becoming the Thought Police of *1984*, but at least we now know Ian's Dungeons & Dragons message board name is Baratheon Gargantua, so who cares?

Kitchenetiquette

Every food-based office scenario is like one of those psychological case studies you read about in college but that probably aren't legal to do anymore. You know, like the one where the guy has to keep pressing a button or else they shock someone? Or is it so they *will* shock someone? Forget it. You know the one we mean. The important thing is, every time food is introduced, it presents an opportunity to judge those around you—and to plumb the depths of your own psyche.

The Candy Dish Test

The desktop candy dish presents an interesting dilemma. Namely, if you want a piece of candy from a coworker's desk, are you obligated to socialize with that coworker? If so, for how long? If you spend double that time engaging in small talk, can you take a second candy? Is a policy of "one for the road" appropriate? Honestly, if the candy keeper is busy, it's probably *less* rude to just take a candy and move along. So go ahead and snatch a fun-size Snickers and keep walking. Or, you could honor the classic Halloween tradition of waiting until the coast is clear and cleaning out the entire stash.

Or, you could, you know, get your own candy dish. But who wants all those other people hovering around your desk like UFOs above drunk farmers' crops? Not you.

The Refrigerator Note Situation

An office setting, unlike a living situation, provides little incentive to tolerate subpar kitchen etiquette. We're reluctant to take a match to the gasoline-soaked rags of our personal lives over issues like cleaning the microwave or stealing a bite from someone's carton of ice cream. We will, however, turn our office kitchen or pantry into a conflagration of unrestrained rage. Notes that would otherwise remain passive-aggressive become *massive*-aggressive when they're directed toward anonymous co-workers rather than specific roommates/significant others/ spouses. A simple "please throw out your expired food" note, after weeks ossifying under the pressure of everyday workplace stress, could very easily become: "Your mother doesn't work here. Toss your own garbage. You're never going to eat that Greek yogurt, *SONYA*."

The office common space is the workplace's seedy under-belly, where transgressions real and imagined provoke feuds and vendettas. Leaving a piece of bread in the toaster can turn a pre-viously cordial relationship chilly. Moving someone's banana can set off a *True Detective*–style investigation that takes violent twists and turns before ending with an unsatisfying whimper.

The measure of your sanity is the degree to which you can resist getting involved in the first place.

The Free Food Conundrum

They say there's no such thing as a free lunch, and in the case of an office luncheon, they are correct. Even when a meal doesn't carry a monetary cost, it takes a vast psychic toll. A work lunch echoes Thomas Hobbes's description of man in a state of nature: nasty, brutish, and short. Catering brings civilization to its knees, with the rush to pick the most desirable sandwich, the juiciest chicken breast, or the least disgusting flavor of diet soda, nearly enough to push a workplace to the brink of anarchy.

More than any other professional scenario, free food reduces us to our basest instincts and reflects what kind of people we are in our moral centers. Watch carefully and you'll learn everything you need to about your coworkers. Who loads up their plate on the first pass through a buffet, intent on providing for himself to the point of satisfaction at any cost? Which colleagues make sure to leave enough for others, bolstering the bodies and the morale of the entire group? Who gets salad like an idiot? Watching people eat is like watching people dance. You see how they move through the world, where they exert their power. And, most important, what their weak points are.

Joe Blew It: Ballin' Out of Control

The recipe for every company softball team is roughly the same. Sprinkle in a few weekend warrior types, social climbers, boozehounds, and bros who take softball more seriously than national security. Then season to taste. Now do a spit-take because it tastes disgusting.

On the corporate softball team I once belonged to, one of my disproportionately enthused coworkers was the (self-appointed) coach. His Gatorade-dumpable moments included begrudging compliance with the league-mandated number of women on the field per inning, and yelling, "Wait for yours!" whenever one of our batters got a strike. Before I started, he somehow heard that I'd played softball at my previous job. He then attempted to recruit me every time we found ourselves in a bathroom together, to the point where it felt like I had a third-base coach guiding me through urination. ("Keep that stream cresting!") Eventually, he wore down my resistance and I joined the team, but as fate would have it, I missed the season opener. Because I was working. At my job. Still, this absence was seen as a betrayal of the highest order. My number one draft pick status curdled into a probationary pledging.

After a weak first showing, I was unceremoniously benched for two games straight. The coach's decision seemed to stem from two parts resentment that I'd missed a game, one part fear that I wasn't actually any good, and 10 percent just being a dick. Again, this was the company softball team, not a professional-sports organization. Second place at a county fair Battle of the Bands would be a bigger deal than our winning every game of the season while blindfolded. Still, this situation seemed to reopen scars from Little League, long ago soothed by competitive sports avoidance and emotional eating. On that third game, I swallowed my pride and asked to play again, before precedent established me as the designated bench rider. The coach kind of made a jerk-off motion with his eyes, but he agreed to put me back on the roster. For a while.

I was uncharacteristically on fire that day. By midway through the game, I had hit a triple, got batted in, and also caught two pop flies. The next time we took the field, however, the coach sotto voce told the guy he'd benched in my stead to run onto the field. When the other team noticed, they made a fuss. With all the power vested in him by the corporate softball association of New York City, our fearless leader yelled out, "Berkowitz, bring it in." To which I replied, "Are you fucking kidding me?" As it turned out, *no*, he was *not* kidding. To my credit, I didn't stand around and wait for this injustice to be sorted out. Instead, I slunk off the field and rolled a softball over a twig with my foot, as if it were an enormous boulder finally crushing Indiana Jones.

The following Monday, I got a call from the *assistant* coach (nobody knew we had an assistant coach) strongly suggesting that the team and I go our separate ways. My outburst was a treasonous fire that had to be snuffed out before spreading into full-blown mutiny. Whether I'd been right to voice my concerns, I'd done so in the wrong way and would now forever be known as the guy who got kicked off his company softball team. It was like fouling out in the end zone. Or dunking from the penalty box. Maybe not. I might be better at describing sports if I'd been allowed to continue playing softball.

YOU'RE GOING PLACES (AT LEAST, PHYSICALLY)

CHAPTER 11

Transportation: Pains, Trains, and Automobiles

People say life is a journey, not a destination—which is weird, since an endless journey is the dictionary definition of purgatory. Whether you're en route to Tahiti or commuting to work, the same kind of people and situations await. The part of travel that billboards don't advertise is how it's an obstacle course full of compromise, tactical evasion, and strangers throwing overfull suitcases at your dreams. When you're out there literally rubbing elbows with people, there are more opportunities per square inch for excruciating mishaps than at any other time. Getting there may be half the fun, but it's also most of the stress, three-quarters the discomfort, and all the butt-crack sweat.

Driving Yourself Crazy

Thanks to GPS technology, teens are far less likely to get lost on a road trip and be subsequently murdered by hook-handed lunatics. The open road is one place that technology has improved across the board. Between air-conditioning, podcasts, and improved fuel efficiency, the only impediment to a smooth commute is (surprise!) traffic. Really, your problem is the other drivers. They change lanes without signaling. They clog up the roads. They rear-end you because they are texting "ttyl" instead of looking where they're going. An accident that is someone else's fault is almost worse than one you cause. In the long run, it may cost you less money, but in the meantime you're stuck in a he said/she said/the police officer failed to write down situation.

Let's Stay Together

Taking public transportation can be less stressful than driving, unless you have to fight to sit next to your traveling companion. Fail to show up early enough for a bus or train trip and there may not be enough empty seats. Some look free as you approach, but upon closer inspection they're occupied by a very short person. A single traveler *voluntarily* sitting with a stranger would be deemed a madman and voted off the bus, so apart from other, more punctual couples smugly sitting with each other, the bus looks like an unevenly distributed egg carton. Now you have to convince two of those eggs to co-egg so you and your companion can, too. This is harder than it sounds.

Blowing it here can not only make you the pariah of the Peter Pan bus, but it can also drive a wedge into your relationship. Nobody *has* to switch seats just because the two of you stopped at Starbucks on the way. Like Blanche DuBois, you're depending on the kindness of strangers—possibly mid–nervous breakdown. Then again, if you're respectful and nobody shows any mercy, perhaps these people deserve a bit of the discomfort they're trying to avoid. At this point, you've got nothing to lose, so digging your heels in isn't the worst thing you can do.

In most cases, it's not that any particular seat is too great to give up. People refuse to move because they think if they stay put, they get to sit alone. They might put a laptop on the tray table of the other seat so it looks like there's another passenger in the bathroom. They might stuff a trench coat full of other trench coats and rig a newspaper on top, giving that imaginary friend a body. Don't let them. Make it clear that you're perfectly willing to plop down next to them—and that it will be awkward as fuck. Nothing keeps you safe like mutually assured destruction.

Leaving on a Jet Plane, Maybe

One sad reality of air travel is that when you most need to get somewhere, everyone else does, too. What you've signed up for is nothing less than a day among a small city's worth of irritable strangers lodged inside a single building. Newark Liberty International Airport is how the poet Dante would have described an outer circle of hell if he'd been alive in modern times and not back in the 1800s or whenever. (Historical accuracy is beyond the scope of this book.)

To maximize the anguish of the friendly skies, start by planning an intricate itinerary that relies on timing and efficiency. Setting a carefully planned travel schedule and trusting an airline to make it happen is like tuning a Stradivarius and then handing it to a toddler in the middle of a tantrum. (Toddlers are terrible at the violin.) The best-laid plans of mice and men, as the saying goes, will be shot to shit when Spirit Airlines gets involved. And if you have a layover, forget it. Airlines love to schedule connecting flights roughly forty-five seconds after your first plane lands. And the second flight never takes off from anywhere near where the first one stops. Why would it? That would be too easy. Every connection you have to make will involve a half-mile sprint, some kind of shuttle bus or monorail (the form of transit restricted to airports, theme parks, and, like, six blocks in Seattle), and maybe even a single-engine prop plane, just to get you to the next terminal. Plus, if you miss the flight, prepare to enjoy a day of fifteen-dollar airport sandwiches and a night in a noisy hotel on your own dime. The fun never ends. ("Fun" in this case being short for "inability for a system to function as promised.")

And all this excitement comes *after* getting through security. That process now includes presenting seven or eight forms of legal identification, stripping down to a sock over your genitals (à la mid-1990s Red Hot Chili Peppers), and standing inside some sort of radiation chamber while confessing the last image you found sexually arousing. These are all very important security measures the government has implemented. They create the illusion that we are somehow *ahead* of any potential terror threats and not subject to the horrors of random and brutal violence that define the world we live in.

To spend the most time trying to get through security, here are a few simple tips:

- Wear lots of metal jewelry, especially hard-to-remove piercings. You'll get sent in circles through the metal detector like it's your partner in a square-dancing class.
- You're going to have to remove your shoes. Wear knee-high boots!
- Forget your passport.
- Bring some kind of dangerous item on board. Items considered dangerous include cigarette lighters, scissors, more than three ounces of toothpaste, a bottle of water, happiness.

Simply walking through the security line affords you the opportunity to get yelled at by a government agent with a clipboard. Oh, my laptop goes in a separate bin? You don't say! Actually, you do say. About a thousand times a day. And all TSA agents treat the line like a single person they've been chastising repeatedly. So any little way you screw up, they respond as though they've been spending the entire morning giving you a one-on-one security tutorial that you ignored. Get ready to be pulled aside for a "random" bag check if you so much as ask a question in the wrong tone. The only way to combat this is to opt out of the body scan and choose a pat-down instead. Then offer to pat the TSA officer down as well. (They all look so lovely!)

Finally, the airplane. Once you're in your seat, don't count on legroom, quiet, snacks, or entertainment. Bring your own laptop or tablet device. Wait until takeoff. Then use it to knock yourself unconscious. Otherwise, you're leaving yourself open to smells, sounds, Vince Vaughn movies, and small talk. Every flight gives you the same forced conversation about where you're from and what you do for a living. It exposes you to the same spectrum of farts and sneezes in which to marinate. You used to be able to smoke in the sky. Because humans have no idea how to do anything right. But hey, maybe you'll get seven pretzels and half a can of soda.

Basically, the entire point of air travel is to make you love the family or business associates you're visiting more by reminding you how much you hate strangers. That and to assure you arrive for your vacation in maximum need of relaxation.

Arm-restling

One day, technology will evolve to the point where commercial aircraft will be able to accommodate every passenger's arms. Both arms! In this utopian dreamscape, our elbows will soar through musty cabin spaces, free as an airplane through the clouds. Until then, on every flight, in every row, somebody is going to get seriously arm-screwed. If you're in the window or aisle seat, the worst that can happen is you'll only get one armrest. Sorry about that. We've started a Kickstarter in your name to build a violin so small that it could play only for you. The poor jerk in the middle seat, however, has a chance of not getting any armrest at all. Unacceptable! Just because you're single and too lazy to buy a ticket until the day before your trip doesn't mean you have no rights. You have at least as many rights as you have arms. Maybe more! There are four ways to approach the arms race.

The Early Bird

If you're the first in your row to arrive, that armrest is yours for the taking. Plunk down an appendage and see what happens. It's a power move that makes late-arriving neighbors either submit to domination or plot revenge.

The Sacrificial Lamb

Some of us were born to be lovers and not fighters. Specifically, we love avoiding furniture-based confrontation. The Sacrificial Lamb surrenders in advance, keeping an arm packed neatly beneath the armrest like a secret weapon of inestimable strength. Who knows—the neighbor may turn out to be one of those weirdos who don't use the armrest, a victory by TKO.

The Boiled Frog

They say it's hard to get a frog to jump into hot water, so the best way to boil that frog is to put it in warm water and slowly turn up the heat. (It was a fine day when the villagers of Frogistan figured this out. They dined on frog porridge until they puked in the streets.) The Boiled Frog is a gradual nudging of the scrimmage line in your neighbor's direction. Perhaps he or she will accept, and perhaps not. It's in God's mysterious hands now.

The Tiger Shark

Of course, some people straight-out attack those two inches of chair like Braveheart being told that kilts are for losers. Snatching a neighbor's armrest when they leave for the bathroom is nothing less than a declaration of war. The Tiger Shark fears no enemy and will fight to preserve his or her land. You can take arm rights, but you can never take arm freedom.

Assault on Battery

From the time you leave home in the morning, your phone is a time bomb, and when the timer (battery level) gets down to zero, your social life, sense of direction, and general usefulness all implode simultaneously. Smartphones have become such a part of our lives that they've muscled digital cameras and GPS devices off of shelves entirely. We all depend on our phones to get from place to place, let people know when we get there, and perform any other function we used to delegate to maps, phone books, guidebooks, our own memories, and advice from our parents.

Guarantee yourself a terrible day by leaving the house with a half-full phone battery. Then forget your charger at home. You'll spend every waking moment prioritizing your communications. Check your e-mail on the half hours, not every nine seconds, like you're used to doing. Keep calls to two minutes or less. (Just kidding. Who makes phone calls?) God forbid you get stuck in a group text message. A group text is a tapeworm for your phone's battery life. When your battery display hits the red, that's the modern "life flashing before your eyes." Time to get your affairs in order. Choose whom you really need to talk to. Be concise and to the point. Get busy living while your battery is busy dying.

In the case that you *do* remember your charger, your day becomes a *Book of Eli*–intense search for a functioning, unoccupied outlet. You will do anything to gain control of one when you find it: barter, plead, lie, engage in a fistfight, or form volatile alliances. The Outlet Miser is one of society's most nefarious figures. He or she has the good fortune to have arrived at the coffee shop or airport while a plug was available, and while your precious battery power dwindles, the Outlet Miser suckles at the benevolent teat of the establishment, A TEAT HE HAS NO OWNERSHIP OVER! You can try to wait out an Outlet Miser, but his vast resources will inevitably outlast you. Your best chance is to find another outlet (even if that means traveling miles) and remembering not to become the very thing you hate once your needs have been fulfilled.

Travel by Numbers

If you're traveling far from home, you need to do more math than usual. Here's a brief rundown of all the little numerical hiccups that could derail an otherwise pleasant trip:

- **Time Zone:** What time is it where you are? What time is it where you came from? If you have loved ones waiting to hear from you, totally ignore the time difference and call whenever is convenient for you. If they have a landline, make sure to use that so you can wake them up if they're asleep.

- **Money:** Don't bother learning conversions if you're leaving the country. Pay with a credit card despite lavish surcharges. Purchase a fistful of local currency and immediately forget how much you spent. Paying ten pounds for lunch seems reasonable at a London café . . . until you realize that you spent nearly twenty dollars on a sandwich.

- **Distance:** Miles? Kilometers? Who cares? You're on vacation!

- **Date:** When are you returning? Great question. There's nothing like jet lag and time off of work to make you forget what day it is. Lose yourself in the moment. Neglect to pay bills. Disregard birthdays.

- **Clothing Sizes:** Shoes are different sizes in seemingly every country. That's a lot to keep track of. Don't. If you're shopping in other countries, just give up. You already can't keep track of what size you are at the Gap versus Old Navy.

Giving Directions and Taking a Loss

Studies say that most accidents happen in or around the home, but most devastatingly awkward encounters happen out in the world. Any interaction that requires you to speak more than two sentences can go horribly awry before you can say, "That's not what I meant!" Specifically challenging are any transactions that require you to give directions—if these go wrong, it's partly your fault. Way to go, dummy!

Riding in a Taxi

Once you've fought through the crowd of other people/selfish nightmares and snagged a taxi—depending on the time of day, a process akin to boxing out an entire street corner of Charles Barkleys for a rebound—that's when the real trouble begins. With the rise of Uber and Lyft, getting a cab is now easier than ever, but, unfortunately, so is getting lost in a cab. Thanks to the more casual "sharing economy" of the 2010s, people don't have to be good at things to do them professionally. Lyft is like an Etsy store on wheels, just a folksy, homespun ride from place to place. Sure, it may not have the same "professionalism" as a real taxi, but you get the charm of taking the scenic route everywhere, and the excitement of a driver punching an address into his phone while driving with his or her knees.

And even though such navigational tools are at the disposal of professional drivers, you can still make them furious by daring to name an address with which they are unfamiliar. Most cabbies in this situation treat you as if you were asking to be driven to the moon. They become incredulous and demand you give them directions with the same intensity that Jack Bauer interrogates suspected terrorists on 24. Here's the catch: Often, when you're in a taxi, you are in an unfamiliar locale, drunk, or both. So your direction-giving may not be at the top of its game. Plus, it's not your job. When you walk into a Best Buy, it is the responsibility of the person in the blue Best Buy shirt to tell you where USB cables are. If he asked you for that information, it would be inappropriate. If he got mad at you for asking *him*, *that* would be ridiculous. Similarly, when you are wearing a taxi as your uniform, you are expected to know where things are, or at least use the "magical computer that you're listening to through a Bluetooth" to figure it out. (Side note: Taxi drivers talk on the phone recreationally more than any other group of people besides moms. Taxi drivers and their mothers must have amazing relationships.)

Mass(ively Unpleasant) Transit

Welcome aboard the subway, one long interactive advertisement for blowing up the subway. Meet your fellow passengers, a 1992 U.S. Olympic dream team of hobgoblins. Folks tucking away pungent home-cooked meals or spitting sunflower shells directly on the floor. iPhones blasting today's Top 40 hits at full volume—as though headphones were just a beautiful sci-fi dream. People clipping their crusty man-talons so that something from their bodies can stay a part of the subway forever. Dudes casually sitting with knees in different zip codes, as though their balls were huge, egg-shaped grenades that detonate upon contact with thigh flesh. People wearing backpacks on crowded cars, the spatial equivalent of giving a moody child a piggyback ride while he shoves other passengers with his tiny hands. And then there's you. You're not off the hook either.

That's right. At any moment on the subway ride to work, you might accidentally thrust your body into somebody else's life. Sometimes you walk in and stop right away, with otherworldly confidence that no one could possibly be behind you—

leaving whoever *is* back there unable to board. You might then go and lean against the metal seat dividers, placing an elbow or butt cheek next to a seated person's jawbone. And if you don't know where you're going, you can closely examine the subway map, causing the person sitting in front of it to keep tilting their head to the side so you can see, until they're convinced this is a German psychological experiment involving neck cramps.

Even when you're trying to do the right thing during a commute, there's a chance you're still a big, oblivious wrecking ball inconveniencing everybody. When a street preacher starts yelling that the day of reckoning is at hand, you might assume the other passengers are wondering when some hero will stand up to this lunatic. They're not thinking that, though. The second you open your mouth to silence one of God's raving children, you become indistinguishable from them. Now the people next to you are worried they're about to witness *true* lunacy, or worse—performance art.

Picture Imperfect

"Take a picture; it'll last longer" was once a sick burn you'd say to anyone you caught staring. The starer would be humiliated, bystanders would pull down their sunglasses and go "Dammnn!" and there'd be much hand-jiving. It was a different time. Nobody imagined that one day every single pedestrian would come equipped with surveillance capabilities. The classic "take a picture" remark is now pointless because by the time you catch people staring, they've already sneakily taken pictures from a variety of angles and aspect ratios, and they're only still staring so they can add contextual sealant to this particular vault in the spank bank. And the *dudes* who do it are even grosser.

Stealth picture taking isn't just the province of perverts anymore, though. Ever since we got camera phones, we have become exhaustive documentarians of foofaraw, celebrating every passing moment like Ken Burns's nemesis, Ken Chills. A pretty sunset, a buttery croissant, two dogs getting it on—all these sights register as Instagram gold. Our days are spent mining reality for material worthy of those unfortunate enough to draw from our shallow streams. All too often during our travels, however, other people become part of the scenery. And getting busted taking pictures of them looks even worse than whatever goofy crap they're wearing.

If you take a picture of someone on the street, he or she might assume you're a confused paparazzo and be flattered. It's the kind of validation that could bring a depressed, vain person back from the brink. But the very thing that makes it tempting to snap candid shots of peacocks on a subway or bus—the close, sustained proximity—also ensures you have nowhere to run when they catch you doing so. There are more ways to get caught than accidentally leaving the flash on. Anyone bold enough to wear a rayon camouflage sweater-vest encrusted with tiny birdbones is aware of who's paying attention. Once he sees how you're tilting your phone toward him and batting your thumb around, your cover is blown. You can try playing it off as though you look at *everything* on your phone at a ninety-degree vertical slant, but Sweater-Vest knows what you're doing, and he's the one staring at you now, until you abruptly get off at whatever the next stop is and build a new life for yourself there.

A Time for Change

Walking to and from work will give you a salty taste of a city's homeless population, one, sadly enough, that serves as a constant reminder of the shits we fail to give about each other. It's true of any city you might visit. We neglect our veterans. We don't provide adequate mental health care. And we take out our animosity toward subway mariachi bands and reckless taxis on homeless people by not giving them money. Because of the taboos involved during any encounter with a homeless person, you are virtually assured of an uncomfortable interaction. But you *can* take that unease and jack it up until it ruins not only your day but the day of everyone around you.

For one thing, judging a homeless person out loud promises to create a real messy scene. It doesn't matter if he lies and says he needs a dollar for a train ticket but you know he's going to use it to buy drugs or booze. Someone is having a shitty day and needs a drink. Way to go, detective. You sleuthed it out. Know who else drinks sometimes? You do. Plus, stop acting like you don't know anyone who has ever bought drugs. Or sold drugs, for that matter. If someone is asking you for money for drugs, he probably needs drugs more than you need to spend five dollars on the Starbucks latte you're guzzling. Just give him the money or don't. Judging out loud is going to start an argument. An argument you can't win. Because once you start shouting at each other, your day is going to get worse a lot faster than his.

But a more mortifying moment is confusing a non-homeless person for a homeless person. It doesn't happen often, but when it does, it's a societal faux pas that's equivalent to asking a woman if she's pregnant, realizing she's not, and following up with: "Good, because you'd be a terrible mother anyway." It's a rare but not impossible mistake to make. Sometimes it's the morning, and you're on a busy street, and a person wearing shabby clothes holding a coffee cup bumps into you, and you have headphones on. And you, not hearing what she is saying, respond: "Sorry. I don't have any change." And then she is like: "I was just saying watch where you're going, asshole. And now you're a double asshole, asshole!" Two people's days instantly ruined! The only winners here are the people who overheard the conversation, who can laugh at you and tell their friends, who can also laugh at you. The only worse mistake we could imagine is if instead of declining to give money, you threw change into the person's open coffee cup, ruining her coffee with your classist assumptions. If you ever do that, the only reasonable follow-up is to throw yourself into traffic.

A brief list of people you should not just assume are homeless:

- Crust punks
- People sitting on the floor of a bus station
- People wearing sweatpants in public
- A guy playing acoustic guitar outside an abandoned RadioShack
- A woman crying on a park bench
- A weekend dad rocking an unseen Bluetooth

- An actor rehearsing lines to himself
- A lonely dog

Given all the stresses of everyday travel, you may think to yourself that it would be easier to never leave home. And you'd be right. Except, if you never left the house, what would you complain about to your significant other?

CHAPTER 12

Entertainment

The term "nerd" has lost all meaning. Not because nerds have become cool. (They have not. If anything, they've become *even nerdier* than previous generations of nerds could calculate.) It's that everyone has become a nerd about something at a time when technology and brands have turned public obsessing into a national pastime. Whether it's the Chicago Cubs or Chumblecore (the understated filmography of the band Chumbawamba), everyone now has the means to pursue his or her passions around the clock. We indulge our interests like competitive eaters snarfing Nathan's hot dogs, all while live streaming the hot dog eating contest on a hat that's also a microwave, and tweeting guesses about who'll be crowned King Sausage Hole.

Each of us has a voice in the cultural conversation, and we use these voices to wolf-whistle at whatever we're stoked about. As overly vocal as we are with online worship, though, we're even more annoying when we venture out into the real world and fanboy all over each other's personal areas. There are things we do in appreciating pop culture that would make all movie stars and football players consider hari-kari, if they weren't profiting obscenely from our appreciation. It seems that one of the requirements for being a nerd about something is making life a living hell for anyone else interested in the same thing.

When Shush Comes to Shove

People are going to talk during movies. It just happens. Sure, there are ads beforehand urging you not to talk, but there are also ads urging you to go see Nicholas Sparks adaptations, and not everybody is doing that either. It's up to you whether the talking ruins the experience. How you handle it has just as much impact on your enjoyment as whether the movie ends with the hero writing a best seller about the events you've just seen, and/ or there's a monkey.

As soon as you hear any voice in the theater that isn't Sandra Bullock's, your ears perk up like NORAD sensors. *Where is it coming from? What is even happening?* You want to take action right away, but there are certain considerations. Taking a hard stance on movie talkers thrusts you into a theatrical spotlight. It turns you into a C-list celebrity of this movie theater, in that everyone is now aware of, and vaguely inconvenienced by, you. Also, no matter how old you are, telling someone to be quiet at the movies immediately thrusts you into middle age and earns you a volunteer position at the local public library.

If you're going to cross that threshold, you'd better be in the right, and you'd better be authoritative. You might be in one of those horror movie crowds where every time something scary happens, six people stand up and yell, "That wasn't scary!" You, the keeper of silence, are in the minority here. If it's just one or two people talking, they have to be involved in a sustained conversational frenzy in order to make you *not* the bad guy for shushing them. Jumping the gun after the people two seats back have only said a few words gives away your moral high ground. Now your date has received the unwanted spoiler that *you* finish poorly.

Thumb War: Texting as an Act of Aggression

Here's a list of various events where texting is disruptive, from least to greatest distraction:

- **Teenager's Birthday:** Literally everyone else is texting.

- **A Nature Hike:** If a man texts in the forest, can anyone hear his keyboard click?

- **Classical Music Concert:** You should be allowed to bring only a rotary phone with you.

- **A Play:** We *get it*. You go to *plays*.

- **Movie Theater:** There are robots exploding on the screen! Look at those!

- **Operating Room:** No, the extra light does not help.

- **Church/Synagogue:** Don't, unless you're texting God.

- **Stand-up Comedy Show:** You're ruining it. Trust us.

- **Loved One's Funeral:** Give it a rest.

- **Your Own Funeral:** Too spooky!

- **The Apocalypse:** Just be in the moment.

To the Victor Go the Spoilers

In olden days, there were only three channels and all anyone watched was *The Tonight Show* with Johnny Carson. Now we have a million cable channels that no one under forty watches because young people pay eight dollars each month for Netflix and the privilege of sneering, "I don't even own a TV." (Feel free to call the most vocal of this bunch IDEOTs.) But because we're in a golden age of television, which sounds like a rumor started by television, you can't expect your friends and acquaintances to have seen any of the same things you have. Therefore, every person lives in constant terror of "spoiling" (a neologism meaning "mentioning") something that someone within a mile radius may not have enjoyed yet.

Others, however, rage against this fear of spoilers. They feel that it's been more than eight years since *The Sopranos* ended, and they should be able to talk about the finale in public without fear of being jumped by a gang of youths who just got HBO GO and are only on Season 2.

If you bring up any piece of entertainment from the past infinity years that contains a plot twist, cameo, or Easter egg in a group larger than two, prepare for someone to chastise you. Then prepare for the chastiser to be chastised. In the present, everyone has a very strong opinion about everything, but everyone resents every other person's opinion. If you *must* bring up a book, song, movie, TV show, cake, or daydream you've enjoyed, write your opinion on a piece of paper, stick the paper in a bottle, write #SpoilerAlert on the bottle, and then throw it into the ocean. Or just write it on your blog. No one reads it anyway.

Otherwise, never talk to anyone about anything.

We Don't Recommend It

In an age of endless entertainment options, a recommendation can feel more like a burden than a favor. It's as if we're already drinking from a fire hose, and *drowning*, then some bro rushes over to describe another hose filled with water that's even wetter.

Recommenders are smug. "Here's a thing you're missing out on in life," is the implication. "Get on the right side of history, you lazy piece of shit." That's right, recommenders are also assholes. They often seem more interested in earning cultural enlightenment badges and advancing to the next level of Couch Potato Boy Scouts. When the following folks recommend this week's white-hot trifle, it puts you in a frantic hurry to go home and never watch it.

Persisters

When people keep following up on a recommendation every time you see them, it forces you to come up with excuses more creative than the movie itself.

Promise Keepers

Some people are so determined to get you to watch a thing that they'll insist on watching it with you, without realizing there is nothing more unpleasant than someone who keeps looking over every two seconds to make sure you're adequately enthused and that you're aware "the good part's coming up."

Backhanders

Sometimes when your friends explain why they think you'll like a certain show, it provides insight into what they think about you altogether. "You'll love this. It's super trashy and everyone in it has an IQ less than 80!" or "This is your jam—you don't have to know about business, politics, or current events to get it!" or "It's like if a cat video was a person and that person was watching a show!"

Long Conners

It's nice when someone says it takes eight or nine episodes to get into a show, because now you know you can get that person to do anything, as long as it takes forever and offers minimal payoff. This is almost certainly how the pyramids were built. "It'll be heavy for the first six or seven years, but then you'll be *hooked* on dragging ten-ton bricks around for days on end under thrash of whip."

Disbelievers

This happens when you freak out because someone hasn't seen *Ferris Bueller's Day Off* and your tenuous grasp on relevance seems to have loosened, and it's all too clear that each of us will one day perish. It's one thing to be surprised when your friend drops a doozy of an absence in her viewing filmography, but some people start flipping cars in the street every time they find out you haven't seen *Backdraft*. Their outrage is supposed to be a recommendation in and of itself—which is a weird way to show that you love something. It's like proposing to a woman by yelling at your friends for not dating her when they had the chance.

Mosh Pit of Despair: The Trouble with Concerts

Just as in life, nobody at a concert is satisfied with the station he or she currently occupies. Unlike life, here you can actually do something about it (something called "shoving"). You push right past whomever you can and disappear into the hydra-headed monster that is the crowd, never to be seen again. Eventually, you make it past someone, but only just so. Like a tired mountain climber, you're forced to make base camp and head for the summit later. Whomever you just shoved moments ago is still closer to you than a Greco-Roman wrestling opponent, and you're each vividly aware of the other's presence. This is the point when someone either spills a drink or projectile sneezes, and the concept of civilization seems like a fairy tale invented by Big Deodorant. Hopefully, you're not at a music festival, though, since those things combine the suck factor of concerts with the sequestering of a grand jury trial. In a Bonnaroo scenario, you run the risk of sleeping in a campsite next to the person who crowded you all throughout My Morning Jacket's set, until you're ready to forget everything Smokey the Bear said about forest arson.

The people who are in your immediate vicinity have the most power over whether you enjoy the show. The band itself comes in a distant second. What good is an unobstructed view if some clumsy jabroni is banging against you like a paddleball? When someone skirts the space between oblivious and intentional with their flying limbs, you might impersonate the town from *Footloose* and threaten to outlaw dancing. The only other choice is to do a revenge Dougie and hip-check that person into the nearest open armpit. Congratulations, you just won your first dance-off!

Overly vocal jerks in concert audiences are as ubiquitous as guitars shaped like pot leaves at 311 shows. There's the guy requesting the same song during every applause break, as though ordering an off-season McRib at a standing-room-only McDonald's. There's the person whose piercing applause-yell sounds like a wolfman at the point of orgasm. These kinds of audience issues are usually resolved with concert karma, though. Obnoxious Yelling Guy will get kicked in the throat by a crowd surfer, iPad Spielberg will get his gear smashed, and anyone who fails at getting a chant going will be haunted by this moment forever.

Stage Fright: The Horror of Watching Your Friends Perform

While the rules for parties/dates/family dinners are all clearly defined, one obligation pales in comparison to the others in terms of full-bodied potential for feeling mortified. We mean, of course, the request to attend a friend's performance.

Receiving such an invitation provokes an onslaught of emotions. First, confusion: *Ted is in a jazz-fusion quartet? Since when?* Then anxiety: *Am I even free that night?* Finally, an overwhelming sense of dread sets in: *Dammit. I am free that night.* A friend's performance is a catch-22. If you don't go, you risk offending someone important to you. If you do go, you have to sit through some art form you may not even like or understand.

Each type of performance comes with its own perils. Your friend's band, for example, might stink. Or, the group might be great but go on at one A.M. in a weird basement of an abandoned church. Or, they might stink *and* perform in that same church basement time slot. A poetry slam may seem like the worst type of event to attend, but remember, every minute you spend listening to terrible poetry yields ten minutes of making fun of it later. Less fertile ground for humor is the first performance of any friend after taking an improv class. Improv is the rare art through which even if your friend is good, he or she will still look bad. Why? Because every first improv show is made up of the following: one weird old guy, two boring nerds trying to become more confident, one loud woman whose friends have convinced her she's "the funny one," six loud men whose friends assured them they're "the funny one," one very nice mom who giggles a lot, and one fat guy who just imitates Chris Farley characters. There is a good chance your friend is one of these people.

As we've mentioned before, the compliment is a delicate art form. And you need to be a true artist when it comes to praising after watching a friend perform. (A real Pablo Picasso.) A handy compliment to give in this situation is: "You were the best one!" It's a way to be nice without lying. Any other pseudo-compliment will be too transparent to function. Feel free to show your friend how you really feel with any of the following:

- "You looked like you were having so much fun!"
- "Good try!"
- "Those chairs were supercomfortable. Sorry I fell asleep."

- "Sometimes it takes a while to figure out what you're good at."

Sports: Where You Can Hate the Player *and* the Game

Sports have saved countless people from death by awkward silence. Yakking about football or the Olympics is the only way many of us can relate to each other, and especially to our dads. In fact, knowing which game is on any given Sunday is equivalent in your father's eyes to building a cabinet or caring about his generation's music. Touchdown! But sports don't always bring together everyone paying attention to them; sometimes they drive the audience apart with the intensity of hyper-trained behemoths gunning for multimillion-dollar bonuses. Here are some of the most likely game day offenders.

Serious Shit-Talkers

Getting crazy aggressive and territorial about someone you'll never know is but one thing sports fans have in common with teens nursing their first celebrity crush. These superfans will loudly defend the object of their affection, even in arguments with confused children (because game recognize game).

One-Fact Wonders

It sucks to be out of the loop, but it sucks even more to shoehorn the single factoid you gleaned from Facebook into a discussion in which everyone else actually knows their stuff. Just keep quiet and maybe you'll learn a second factoid for the next time this happens.

Dress-Code Deniers

A picture says a thousand words, and when you wear a LeBron jersey to your cousin's wedding, that picture says "Go Cleveland!" and then just the word "dickbag" 998 times. Also, if you show up to, say, any bar in Philly wearing a Giants jersey, you might have an awkward conversation... with the EMTs who carry you out of the place.

Sports Grinches

Detachment is a good look. That's why models' faces never betray knowing that cameras are taking their pictures. Distancing yourself from the crowd at a Super Bowl party, though, is not exactly fashionable. You may think dismissing the game as "sportsball" is what a bon vivant in 1920s Paris would do—and who knows, you may be right—but those people are dead now.

Museums: They're *Almost* Fun!

The greatest trick our education system ever pulled was sending us on field trips to museums, thereby convincing us that museums are great by virtue of their being better than school. They also tricked us into thinking that *musea* (definitely not how you pluralize that) are all basically the same. When you go to a museum, you may see beautiful, photo-realistic landscape portraits, or you could end up walking through row after row of old Greek bucket halves. Plus their rules are arbitrary. In some *musaeiou,* you can't take pictures of the artwork, but you can sketch it. That's the same thing, but slower. It's nonsense.

When you're traveling, a museum is a great way to experience local culture without trying any food or seeing diverse neighborhoods or talking to local people. In your own town, visiting a museum allows you to feel smart, even if you learn literally nothing. Using leisure time for a museum visit is like buying a Gucci bag. It doesn't make you *better,* but it does send the message that you're *better than other people.*

If you choose the wrong museum, every moment feels like time spent in detention. Even kinds of art museums vary widely. Almost everyone can recognize a sculpture as "a thing people like looking at." Modern art, however, is less straightforward. Modern art is like butt stuff; if you're not *way* into it, you probably don't like it at all. On the plus side, modern art is an unparalleled instigator for a shouting match with your spouse about whether several jars of scabs count as "art" or whether someone who spent their adult life drawing variously colored and sized squares was a genius.

That's the brilliance of a museum visit. It makes you passionate about stuff you'd never thought about before. Passionate enough to scream at your best friend. Now that's edutainment!

Phone Is Where the Heart Is

Allow us to set a scene, if you will:

It's date night. You and your beloved gaze amorously at one

another across a candlelit table. It's that warm, lovely part of the meal when you've had half a glass of wine and no food. You haven't even thought about which one of you is going to fake offer to pay the check, and who is going to actually do it. It's the kind of place where they grind fresh pepper onto your meal, as if pepper that's a minute old is topsoil. You sigh a sigh of great contentment. A quartet of violins comes to a crescendo.

Then, a faint buzz. Your beloved reaches into his pocket or her purse. Both of your faces fall.

"Let me answer this real quick."

Your beloved responds to the text. Receives a reply. Responds to that. You pull out your own phone. No texts. No e-mails. You put it away, eat your salad. Your entrée comes.

"Sorry. Just this one more."

You finish your meal. Down a second glass of wine. Scarf down both halves of the dessert you planned to split.

Fall turns into winter. Winter turns to spring. Spring gives way to the sweltering summer heat. Your clothes have gone out of style. You've lost touch with your friends. Ironically, you're eligible for an upgrade on your phone.

"I'll be right with you. It's a work thing."

But you don't hear these words. You've been dead for thirty years.

Most of us foster unhealthy attachments to our phones. We respond to their every vibration and Black Eyed Peas ringtone, even when we're in the presence of people we like better than whoever is calling us (not to mention the Black Eyed Peas). We allow everyone in our lives instant access to us because we expect the same from them. If you send a text and it goes unanswered for ten minutes, you freak the hell out. Admit it. If you don't get a response after thirty minutes, your brain quickly declares: "He better be stuck under a pile of boulders!"

Prioritizing your phone over the people in your immediate vicinity is a great way to say: "You know who I like more than you? Everyone." It's a social power grab, but if you fight fire with passive-aggressive fire ("sure, burn that down, don't even ask me") and pull out your own phone when your companion does, you're downloading a white flag of relationship surrender app. Your friendship or romance has been reduced to a reverse staring contest, seeing who can avoid looking at the other the longest. The worst move of all is to call the other person out on his behavior. Why? Well, as soon as you do, he will recite the litany of times when you did *the exact same thing to him*. Because make no mistake, your dining companion has a catalog of grievances time- and location-stamped like *Law & Order* scenes. Voilà! You've ruined date night without even standing up!

CHAPTER 13

The Goods, the Bads, and the Services

Hiring someone to do anything you can do yourself is embarrassing. It's even more humiliating to pay for something you can't do for yourself but *should* be able to. Changing your oil is a very basic task, or so we've heard. We've never tried it. We always avert our eyes and hand our mechanics a small amount of cash to pour goop into one of our car's mysterious car-holes. But really, every transaction comes with its own set of unwritten rules, which are easy to violate without ever knowing what they are. Whether you're trying to buy a couch from a stranger or schedule an appointment to get your taxes done, good luck, and may society have mercy on you.

Body Shop: The Unimaginable Stress of Being Touched

Wherever we may go, one fact always holds true: We hate the touch of strangers. Sometimes, however, we must pay people we've never met to make contact with our bodies in order to make ourselves presentable to society at large. We need haircuts and manicures and the occasional massage—no matter how emotionally exhausting we find them.

Getting a haircut, like peeing in the woods, is less complicated for men. A man can basically walk into any building containing scissors (including slaughterhouses and elementary schools), pay a guy in an apron twenty dollars, and walk out looking decent. A woman, however, often has a more intimate relationship with her stylist. She can't just saunter into any salon. She needs to get a recommendation from a friend and then conduct several interviews. She needs photographic evidence of previous haircuts that a stylist has given. It is a less arduous process to join the Crips or the Illuminati.

Even if you have a hairdresser you trust, it's easy to get a bad haircut. Think of all the dumb haircuts you see walking around all day. Some of those were accidents. Bringing in a picture of the style you want works pretty well, but just as you can't be sure two people see the color blue in the same way, it's impossible to know that you and your hairstylist see the same shape when you look at a photo of your desired do.

The main problem with bringing in a picture is that it can't be a photo of someone who is outrageously better-looking than you. Sure, Colin Farrell has great hair, but if you bring in a picture of him, your barber may comment on how you clearly want to look like Colin Farrell in *every* way, even though no matter what magic transpires in this rotating chair today, it's not gonna happen. That's just sad. You're better off bringing in a picture of a famous person who is perhaps not your cosmetic ideal. Joe, for instance, always asks his barber for "the F. Murray Abraham."

Josh Blew It: Massage Sabotage

I have had only one massage in my life, and I did it wrong. I lay down, fully clothed, on the table as the masseuse went to work with a force that I can only describe as vengeful. Within seconds, my body had grown so tense that I had to be reminded to breathe, and the masseuse felt compelled to tell me that I was "going to be okay." That is a reminder you want during war, not a relaxation experience. I was too ashamed to tell her that she was doing more harm than good. I thought that's how massages were supposed to feel. Even though she had no idea how to make my body feel good, I told her it was going great. It was like prom night.

Mercifully, the massage lasted only fifteen minutes (or, 7.5 prom night sexes), and I managed to limp away before she tore any muscles fully away from my bones. Still, for the rest of the afternoon I felt like I'd run a marathon without burning any calories (unless there were previously unknown caloric benefits to recoiling from the painful touch of a dominatrix).

I went in with some knots in my neck, and when I left my entire body was as impossibly wound as a headphone cord that has been in your pocket for days. I knew, at that moment, that I would never pay anyone to touch my body again.

Bad Medicine

Seeking medical attention is a basic human right, but it's also a terrifying ordeal that makes many adults swallow ibuprofen like breath mints for weeks on end. The longer you wait to access a physician, the more likely you are to be diagnosed with: "Your torso is now entirely occupied by a colony of bees!" or "Your blood has somehow been replaced with Guy Fieri's Donkey Sauce!" For the most unpleasant experience possible, wait until you feel/look like a *Walking Dead* extra before beginning the complicated process of seeing a doctor. And remember: This is America. Make sure to make an in-network appointment. If you just show up at a hospital, you will be charged roughly a zillion dollars for the privilege of waiting for six hours in a room full of people spurting blood and pathogens into the air like sprinklers on a golf course fairway.

Once you see a doctor, it's important to lie, so you look like less of a degenerate. "How long have you been having these symptoms?" your doctor might ask. Instead of being honest and admitting it's been three weeks, but you thought you might have just had an exceptionally long hangover so you've been self-medicating with home fries and naps, just lie and say, "Since late last night." Not only will your doctor get the (untrue) impression that you're a responsible adult, but you're also shortchanging yourself of the best possible care. Same goes for questions about how often you have unprotected sex, how heavily you use drugs, and how frequently you exercise. You could come clean and get the best medical advice for your lifestyle. *Or*, you could tell a few fibs and continue running your life ashore like some kind of idiot whale.

It's Not Working Out

Personal trainers say showing up is the hardest part of working out at the gym. Not true! The real hardest part is crying while looking in the mirror because your body still resembles a sack of russet potatoes. Dealing with your issues at the gym is stressful enough, even if you aren't doing it surrounded by people whose muscles look like ghosts trying to escape their bodies. Something about the quest to get CGI abs turns way too many of us into a body part reserved for waste (the butthole!).

Let's go back to those trainers. As Socrates taught his pupil Plato, so, too, do these buff professors of fitness attempt to mold you in their own shredded images. In trying to win you over, though, they accidentally insult you, offering to "put a Chunnel-size thigh gap between those doughy calzones of yours," or worse. Even when complimenting your progress, they don't seem to recognize the delicate psyche of an insecure person. They think they're doing you a favor by letting you know you've come a long way and now look less likely to be the first one killed in a combat situation.

At least those people are trying to help, in their own oblivious way. Some folks treat other gym members as if they were day laborers looking for nonunion landscaping work in front of Home Depot. They try and recruit you into spotting them, which means hovering over a horizontal Hulkazoid and shouting, "It's all you, bro!" a thousand times, as he hoists rounded hunks of cast iron skyward, like they're baby Lion Kings. Other gym rats act as if the equipment is New York City's hottest nightclub and you're the bouncer preventing them from getting inside. They ask how many sets you have left, and any amount is too many. No matter your answer, they also want to know whether they can work in with you. But any response other than loudly sighing while giving up the equipment might earn you a gym-esis, whom you will trade glares with on every future visit. (A "gym-esis" is a gym nemesis, not a gymnasium-themed Genesis cover band. Although we could get into that.)

Joe Blew It: Don't Sweat All Over the Small Stuff

There are certain rules to using a gym's cardio equipment. These rules forbid members from wearing jeans, making a mess, or being a turbo-creep. The most enforced of these rules, though, is that second one, which is why I clean my treadmill after a workout until it's "hospital corners" immaculate. You could *eat* off a treadmill after I'm done with it—if, say, you were visiting from Japan and missed having food that comes on a conveyor belt, or are just really eccentric. (There are a lot of ways to live life.) But not everyone using these hamster toys is as dedicated to proper gym hygiene.

One time, I was running like a maniac, and I didn't really notice the guy next to me until he was gone. That's when I saw the tremendous globs of sweat he'd left behind on the machine. It was everywhere. His bodily fluid. Just a *stupid* amount of sweat distributed in chaotic puddles like sad clouds, and it was mostly on the side of the treadmill closest to me.

Just then, a woman in Lululemon regalia strode down the crowded row of cardio equipment toward the empty treadmill next to me. Clearly, she was going to see what this well-hydrated hell-beast had just done and assume I was responsible. I could jump off and start cleaning it up, but that would be weird. No. Instead of that, a simple explanation would do. Because that wouldn't be weird at all.

"Excuse me," I said, as the woman, who was just trying to live her life, neared the empty treadmill. "I gotta say, that's not *my* sweat." Instantly, I realized my mistake. She would never in a million years have cared whether that was my sweat. It only felt that way because the gym makes you super self-conscious about your body and what comes out of it. Not only did I now look like a person who sweats all over cardio equipment, but I also seemed like someone who lies about it. The look of horror in her eyes was not insubstantial. And as she walked out of my life forever, the idea of running away from this awful moment forever became my thinspiration.

Shop till You Stop

The desire to be left alone and make financial decisions in peace is what leads to most awkward shopping encounters. You walk into Hollister, agenda-less, save for a general sense of wanting to be a better-looking person. Right away, the sales staff is at your side, offering to help you find anything you need. Little do they know how much you *wish* there was a specific garment they could locate that would slake the dark hunger inside you.

The problem with having a Scooby to your Shaggy on this fabrics-based mystery is that now there's an 80 percent chance you're going to have to *fire* Scooby-Doo. Zoinks! It's not like at Trader Joe's, where you can just sort of tune out the cashier who's been trained to mention how your Soy Creamy reminds him of a cool textile exhibit at the museum. You can't leave a clothing store empty-handed without telling the person trying to help you that this collaboration has been a failure. So instead you buy the wrong puka shell necklace just so some salesperson will be proud of himself.

When you are looking for help, though, just make sure you ask somebody who actually works there. Mistaking one of your fellow shoppers for sales staff is like a flashback to childhood, when you thought every adult was one of your parents. But instead of cute, people now think you're an asshole.

Tip, Tip . . . Hooray

What even *is* a tip? Is it a bonus for an exceptional experience? Or is it an extra 20 percent you cough up so that you can eat spit-free food and avoid a fight with your significant other over what a stingy monster you are? Whatever your philosophy on tipping, it's unlikely that your dining party and your server will share a point of view. Leaving gratuity is like lovemaking: It's hard to find someone who feels exactly the same as you do, and no matter what anyone says, it's never *just* about the tip.

Throwing down a giant tip makes you look like a cocky jerk; tossing a five-dollar bill into a change cup is an expensive way to announce that you are a show-off who doesn't budget well. Under-tipping is a far more efficient way to reveal to the world that you're terrible. But don't wait until the check comes. Talk loudly about how you don't *believe* in tipping and how in Europe *nobody* tips. Ignore how woefully inadequate the wage for servers is. Quote Ayn Rand to your friends. Get more passionate about it than you do about any other political issue. If you don't have change on hand, don't ask for it. Bartenders/baristas hate making change. They hate it even more than having health insurance and paying rent. You're putting them out. Don't bother them with your tip.

Go Big, Then Go Home: A Brief Guide to Tipping

Here is a guide to acceptable tipping amounts that will make you seem classy. If you tip less than these quantities, you are basically an urban libertarian, the smuggest and least enjoyable type of person.

- **Sit-Down Meal:** 20 percent, even if the service is not good. *Yes, we said it.*

- **Coffee:** Throw any change (coins) into the cup unless you're a real dick.

- **Full-Service Gas Stations:** You don't tip at all for some reason. This one's a puzzler. Who decided that the majority of gas station employees are secret millionaires who just love pumping gas?

- **Bars:** Tip one dollar per beer/wine. Two per booze drink. Otherwise, don't expect to get your next round anytime this millennium. Bartender's revenge, they call it. (They don't, but they could start.)

- **Taxis:** Start with two dollars. Subtract a quarter for every time the driver endangers your life. Add a quarter every time the driver endangers someone else's life on your behalf.

- **Hotels:** Leave a couple of dollars on the dresser. Yes, that's also how you pay a sex worker, but there's no better way to get cash directly to the people who do the gross job of cleaning up after your sloppy, disgusting vacation self.

- **Delivery:** Five-ish dollars if you're ordering for multiple people, with extra money added if you got delivery because the weather is terrible or it's a holiday when restaurants are super busy. Have some compassion, you filthy animal.

Real Estate, Real Problems

It's hard to believe real estate agents still exist. Seems like we should've evolved past them by now, like we did with travel agents. (RIP travel agents; may you find that elusive connecting flight to heaven.) But for now, at least, society is not ready to revert to handshake deals for housing. The basic process of finding shelter remains insanely complicated.

When an agent shows you someplace that seems livable, you'd be willing to compete in the Hunger Games to get it, if only to enjoy less cutthroat competition. That's how personal the process feels—like anyone looking at the same listing is trying to throw you out on the street to die of rat scabies. When you are at a potential new home, the last thing you want is for the agent to double-book the time slot. It's a reminder that nobody is pulling for you—that each of us eventually dies alone, but the person looking at you right now is actively hoping you lose your job and your brother rips you off in some pyramid scheme and you have to live in a tree house. All you can do is stand there and look around the place and perhaps announce phony structural flaws to discourage your new blood enemy from putting in an offer.

Even if no other potential buyers are around, things can still easily go FUBAR. There's no graceful way, for instance, to use the bathroom in a house you're considering buying. It's widely known that taking a dump in a potential home is a declaration of your very serious intent to buy. If that's not the message you're trying to send, you now have to send an opposite message through real estate code: by gathering the dining room's entire contents into a tablecloth hobo bindle, and planting it in the front yard like a flag.

Asking questions about the house is your chance to shine, and by "shine" we mean "be mistaken for a racist murderer." It's hard to ask about how "nice" a neighborhood is, for instance, or the noise level, without seeming like you're fishing for certain answers. The question "What kind of people live around here?" can be taken a lot of ways, but it mostly sounds like you're requesting a book of mug shots or a menu for cannibals.

"What Do You Mean There's No Bathroom?"

So many things agents say, either in person or in listings, seem like tiny strain tests for just what you'll believe. Sometimes you have to decipher what they're really saying.

Here are some standard Q&A's

Q. How many square feet is "larger than it looks"?

A. Larger than the picture looks. Because it's a building, not a picture. But still super small.

Q. **What is a "desirable neighborhood"?**
   A. Desired by Godzilla for eating. Because Godzilla only eats literal toxic garbage.

Q. **What is a "carpenter's dream"?**
   A. Sometimes when carpenters have a hard time providing for their families, they dream of a building so poorly constructed that it will require unlimited jobs until the end of time. Saddest dream ever.

Q. **What does "lots of living space" mean?**
   A. Very few corpses!

Q. **What is a "motivated seller"?**
   A. One classic motivation is living next to a tire fire.

Q. **Just how "quaint" and "retro" is this place?**
   A. It was once visited by Mary Todd Lincoln.

Q. **What "recent renovations" are there?**
   A. One room is now a fishery.

Q. **Why is it a "fixer-upper"?**
   A. It will fix your wallet from having money.

Credit-Check Yourself Before You Credit-Wreck Yourself

The most awkward time to deal with a real estate agent is when you're a young couple. Most agents have been around the block—literally, one would hope—and they know love can be a fickle thing. As much as they'd like to take your collection of money, they also want to make sure you're aware of the risks.

That's why young couples sometimes end up having to assure real estate agents of their sturdiness. They field questions about their future together and it's as invasive as if, after helping them land an apartment, the agent showed up to make sure the cohabitation was properly consummated. Unfortunately, the best way to assure an agent you're ready is by not fighting during the home-hunting process—which is difficult because nothing makes couples fight more than looking for an apartment.

Getting Friends to Help You Move: A Timeline

Two Weeks Before Move: Post status update on Facebook offering pizza and beer for friends willing to help you move.

Three Days Before Move: Desperately reach out to three friends who owe you the most favors and cash in.

Day of Move:

8:00 A.M.: Talk shit about friend who didn't show up to two friends who did.

8:03 A.M.: First time you order a friend around like you're his actual boss.

9:15 A.M.: Friend accidentally hits your shin with a table leg and you try not to scream at him.

11:25 A.M.: Instead of yelling, "Get back to work!" you work twice as hard to make your friends, who are on an extended smoke break, feel bad for not helping.

11:45 A.M.: Realize plan backfired so hard.

1:30 P.M.: Yell at friend for dropping something expensive.

1:32 P.M.: Drop something expensive.

2:24 P.M.: Your surprisingly robust sex toy collection makes its public debut.

4:48 P.M.: "Dude, are you serious right now? Get back to work!"

6:32 P.M.: Your friend remarks how "cozy" your tiny apartment looks. You begin to wonder if perhaps you made a huge mistake.

8:50 P.M.: You're informed that your promise of pizza includes lunch, dinner, *and* pizza rolls. While you run to the store, your sex toy collection makes its hilarious second appearance.

1 Day Later: Begin extensive search for new best friends.

Epilogue

So you've made it all the way to the end of our book. Wow, that's a lot of time to spend reading about uncomfortable silences and drunk texts. We're impressed and creeped out. If you like us so much, why don't you marry us? Seriously, at least consider it—Josh needs *two* green cards somehow, and Joe's just a really big fan of weddings.

Now that you're more aware of the spirit-crushing pitfalls that perforate each day, you probably feel ready to take on the world and tame it like a circus lion. You see the matrix—and not just because *The Matrix* is on the TBS Sunday Afternoon Movie Train. The prospect of an unreturned high five now enters your head before your hand even goes up, not unlike Neo uploading karate-GPS into his brain and knowing just where his opponents' crane kicks will land. You intuitively sense the dangers you only recently discovered, and then you put your hand back in your pocket, where it's safe. Everything's going to be hunky-dory from now on, right?

Wrong. It's not just suddenly going to be all right, you poor, naive, exceedingly well-read son of a gun. What you don't know about life's social land mines could just about fill up a book. Another book, besides this one. And one that's not quite as good.

Simply knowing about all the embarrassing things you might do won't stop you from doing them. Not at all. Even though you read this whole book—and ugh, seriously, why don't you and the book get a room?—you're no more likely now to do any better at interacting with peers and strangers and minor celebrities paid to make appearances at Foxwoods Resort Casino. All this information is lodged in your head now, and it's poisoning your brain. It doesn't matter that we've been ushering you in the direction of avoiding awkwardness. If we (Joe and Josh) were to say, "Don't think of an elephant," guess what would happen? *Boom*—you're majoring in elephant.

Take Joe, for instance (and again, are your marriage prospects really so stellar that you can count him out?). Joe overthinks everything and then manifests the worst possible outcome, just by being aware of it. His signature move is coming up with exactly the wrong thing to say, patting himself on the back for not saying it... and then saying it. And to answer your question, *yes*, he *has* ruined a surprise party before.

When you think of Murphy's Law, think of us (Josh and Joe)—and also maybe a sitcom about a circuit court judge named Murphy whose courthouse is *always* out of order. If anything can get blown, it will. And despite the tragic recession that has beset the inner-tube industry in recent years, something can always get blown. Don't say you weren't warned.

But, if it makes you feel any better... everyone else is blowing it, too.